from FIRST JOB to LEADERSHIP

The Ultimate ATS and AI Resume Guide

AF438349

APARAJITA SUDARSHAN

ISBN
Paperback 979-8-89673-805-3
Hardcase 979-8-89724-500-0

CONTENTS

ABOUT THE AUTHOR

Aparajita Sudarshan is a seasoned professional with over 17 years of rich and diverse experience across multiple industries and countries, including India, UAE, Bahrain, Qatar, Malaysia, and now the UK. Having worked and lived in these vastly different regions, she has gained firsthand insights into the unique challenges of job searching in various cultural and professional landscapes. Each country's interview process presented its own complexities, and Aparajita had to navigate them independently, often through trial and error.

Frustrated by the lack of comprehensive guidance and dissatisfied with expensive, limited subscription platforms, she embarked on a personal mission to demystify the art and science of crafting resumes that stand out. With the rise of AI, she recognized a new challenge—getting past Applicant Tracking Systems (ATS). Despite being highly qualified, candidates often face months of silence, with their resumes failing to align with rigid ATS criteria. This realization led Aparajita to conduct extensive research, experimenting with countless strategies and tools.

Her journey uncovered a critical truth: no single method is foolproof. The key lies in blending the precision of AI with the creativity and insight of human effort. Through this book, Aparajita shares her hard-earned knowledge, aiming to help others avoid the struggles she faced. With her unique perspective, deep expertise, and passion for empowering job seekers, she hopes to guide readers toward building resumes that don't just meet ATS requirements but also resonate with recruiters, ultimately opening doors to career opportunities worldwide.

By combining her global experience, research-driven insights, and a desire to give back, Aparajita Sudarshan has created a resource that bridges the gap between technology and human ingenuity, empowering job seekers to take control of their futures.

FROM FIRST JOB TO LEADERSHIP: THE ULTIMATE ATS AND AI RESUME GUIDE

Ode To My Readers

In the whirlwind of ruthless emails,
Rejections unspoken, where spirit derails.
Keywords, not skills, the ATS demands,
Dreams slipping fast through merciless hands.
To craft a resume, confusion's art,
Platforms aplenty, they tear you apart.
A loser's shadow, a mind torn in plight,
To write or not, where begins the fight?

Then emerges a guide, a beacon of light,
No false promises, just pathways bright.
Step by step, it clears the haze,
With AI tools and human ways.
Learn the craft, claim your throne,
Turn silence to calls, let success be known.
From despair to interviews lined with cheer,
The future unfolds, your victory near.

With every page, a strength renewed,
Tools in hand, success pursued.
Not just a resume, but triumphs won,
Confidence blooms as the journey's begun.
This is the map to your dream's embrace,
Transforming the odds in this competitive race.
Own this guide and let your power ignite,
Your dream job awaits; take charge tonight.

By – Aparajita Sudarshan

ACKNOWLEDGMENT

With immense gratitude, I thank God for the countless opportunities that have come my way. While many have ended in failure and only a few in success, each experience—success or otherwise—has been a stepping stone toward growth and self-discovery. Every challenge has taught me invaluable lessons and refined my journey, making life one of the greatest teachers.

I dedicate this book to my parents, **Mrs. Swagata De and Mr. Anup Kumar De**, whose unwavering guidance and belief in me have been the foundation of my resilience and strength. Their empowerment has not only enabled me to find my own path but has also instilled in me the ability to empower others.

To my husband, **Mr. Sudarshan Ravindran**, your steadfast support and encouragement have been a pillar of strength throughout this journey. Your belief in my endeavours has made all the difference.

Finally, my hope is that this book serves as a source of guidance and inspiration, helping millions of readers navigate their challenges and unlock new opportunities. To everyone who believes in bettering themselves, this book is for you.

PREFACE: THE RESUME REVOLUTION

The evolution of resume writing has been significant over the years. With advancements in AI, the job market has shifted, emphasizing the need for personalized, data-driven resumes. This guide provides practical steps to integrate AI tools effectively into resume building, balancing automation with human authenticity.

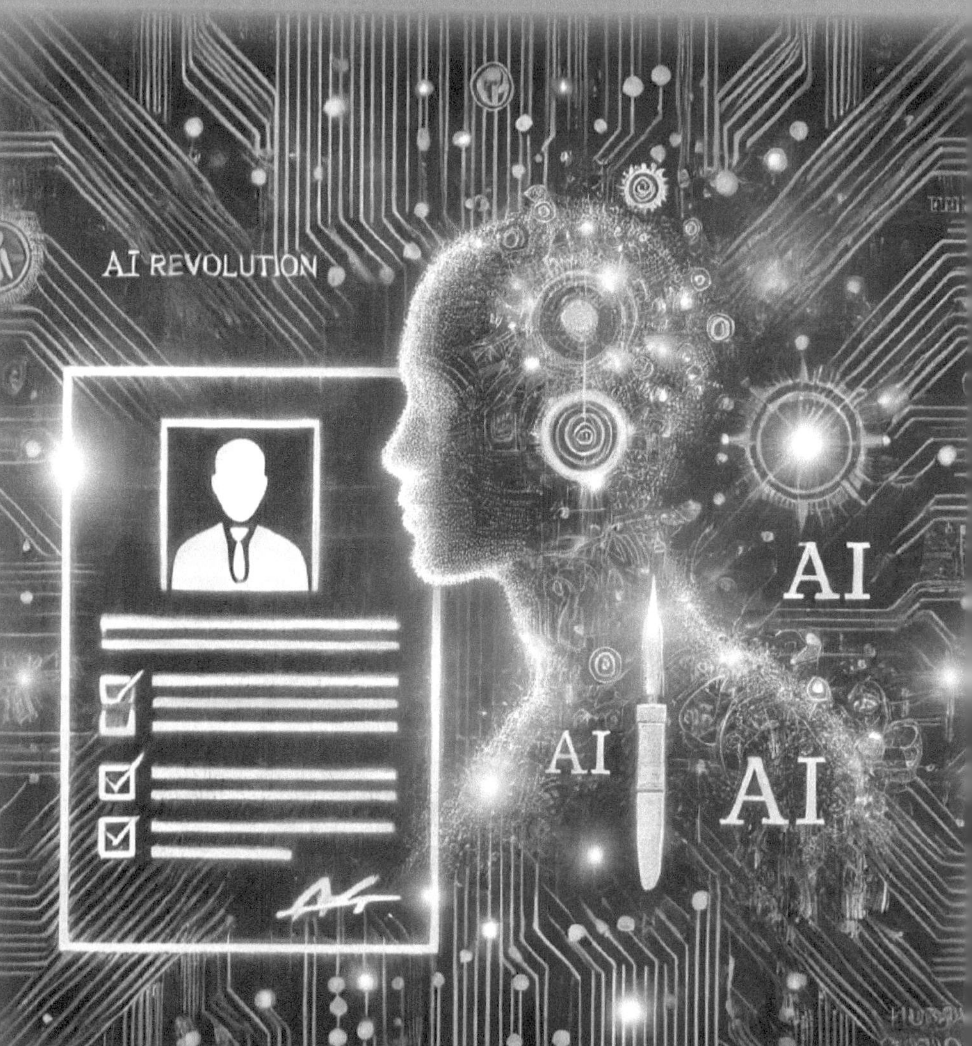

AI REVOLUTION
AI
AI
AI

THE AI REVOLUTION IN RESUME WRITING

In today's hyper-competitive job market, your resume is no longer just a document - it's your digital handshake, your first impression, and often your only chance to catch a recruiter's eye. Welcome to the era of AI-powered resume writing, where cutting-edge technology meets personal branding to create a compelling narrative of your professional journeys.

The Evolution of Resumes: From Da Vinci to AI

Resumes have come a long way since Leonardo da Vinci penned the first known professional letter in 1482. Let's take a quick journey through time: 1950s-1970s: The typewriter era standardized formats.

1980s-1990s: Personal computers revolutionized resume creation.

2000s: Digital job boards and initial Applicant Tracking Systems (ATS) emerged.

2010s-2020s: AI and personalization take center stage. Today, resumes are dynamic, tailored presentations of your skills and achievements.

Compare these examples: Traditional: "Managed a sales team." Modern: "Led a 10-member sales team to achieve a 25% increase in revenue over six months, resulting in $500,000 additional profit. "The difference is stark - it's like comparing a black-and-white photo to a vibrant, high-definition image.

The Modern Job Market Challenge

Today's job seekers face a gauntlet of challenges:

- Global Competition: You're competing with talent worldwide, not just locally.
- Specialized Roles: Generic resumes don't cut it when companies seek niche skills.
- Picky Recruiters: Hiring managers want resumes tailored to their specific needs.
- Time Crunch: Recruiters spend an average of just 6-8 seconds scanning a resume

Here's a sobering statistic: over 75% of resumes are rejected before a human even sees them. Why? Enter the Applicant Tracking System (ATS).

The ATS Gatekeeper

Think of ATS as the bouncer at an exclusive club. It scans resumes for:

- Keywords matching the job description
- Standard formatting and headings
- Relevant skills and experiences

If your resume doesn't have the right "password" (keywords), you're not getting in. But don't worry, AI is here to help you crack the code.

AI to the Rescue: Top Free Tools for Resume Writing

i   ChatGPT: Your Personal Resume Writer

- Strengths: Contextual content generation, experience description, keyword optimization
- Best for: Crafting compelling bullet points and tailoring your resume to specific job descriptions

- Example: Input: "Describe my experience as a project manager"

Output: "Led cross-functional teams to deliver 5 high-impact projects, resulting in 30% increase in operational efficiency and $2M in cost savings."

ii   LinkedIn Resume Builder

- Strengths: Professional networking integration, industry-specific formatting
- Best for: Creating a resume that aligns with your LinkedIn profile
- Tip: Use the "Skills & Endorsements" section to identify key keywords for your industry

iii   Grammarly

- Strengths: Advanced language refinement, writing quality enhancement
- Best for: Polishing your resume's language and eliminating grammatical errors
- Pro Tip: Use Grammarly's tone detector to ensure your resume strikes the right professional tone

iv   Canva AI Resume Tools

- Strengths: Design-focused, vast template variety
- Best for: Creating visually stunning resumes that stand out
- Feature Highlight: Use Canva's Magic Resize to quickly adapt your resume for different platforms (e.g., LinkedIn, email attachments)

v   Hugging Face Open Models

- Strengths: Multilingual support, advanced customization
- Best for: Tech-savvy users looking to leverage cutting-edge AI models

- Example Use Case: Use BERT-based models to analyze job descriptions and extract key requirements

Practical Example: AI in Action

Let's see how AI can transform a bland resume bullet point:
Before: "Increased team efficiency."
After AI Magic: "Boosted team efficiency by 35%, reducing project turnaround time from 6 weeks to 4 weeks and saving the company $75,000 annually through streamlined processes and automated reporting. "Now that's what we call a resume glow-up!

The Human Touch: Why AI Isn't Everything

While these AI tools are impressive, remember they're meant to enhance your resume, not replace your unique voice. Here are some tips for maintaining authenticity:

- Use AI suggestions as a starting point, then customize them to reflect your personal experience.
- Always fact-check AI-generated content. It might suggest skills or achievements you don't actually have.
- Read your resume aloud after using AI tools. Does it sound like you? If not, tweak it until it does.

Looking Ahead: The Future of AI in Resume Writing

As AI technology advances, we can expect even more sophisticated resume tools. Imagine:

- Predictive AI suggesting career moves based on your skills and industry trends.
- Virtual Reality resumes allowing candidates to showcase their skills in immersive environments.
- AI-powered interview prep tools that analyze your resume and generate likely interview questions.

Your AI-Powered Job Search Journey Begins

As we dive deeper into the world of AI-assisted resume writing, remember: the goal is to create a resume that's not just a list of jobs, but a compelling narrative of your professional journey. These AI tools are your sidekicks in this adventure, helping you craft a resume that not only passes the ATS test but also captivates human recruiters. In the following chapters, we'll explore each aspect of AI-powered resume writing in depth, from mastering ATS optimization to crafting compelling narratives that showcase your unique value proposition. We'll also delve into ethical considerations, future trends, and advanced techniques to stay ahead in the ever-evolving job market. Are you ready to give your resume a high-tech makeover? Your dream job awaits, and with AI by your side, you're better equipped than ever to land it. Let the resume revolution begin!

Key Points from Chapter 1: The AI Revolution in Resume Writing

i Evolution of Resumes

- From Leonardo da Vinci's first professional letter in 1482 to today's AI-powered resumes
- Transition through typewriter era, personal computers, digital job boards, and now AI-driven personalization

ii Modern Job Market Challenges

- Global competition
- Specialized roles requiring tailored resumes
- Recruiters spending only 6-8 seconds on initial resume scan
- Over 75% of resumes rejected before human review due to Applicant Tracking Systems (ATS)

iii AI Tools Revolutionizing Resume Writing

- ChatGPT for contextual content generation and experience description
- LinkedIn Resume Builder for professional networking integration
- Grammarly for language refinement and error elimination
- Canva AI Resume Tools for visually appealing designs
- Hugging Face Open Models for advanced, multilingual customization

iv AI's Impact on Resume Quality

- Transformation of bland statements into compelling, quantified achievements
- Example: "Increased team efficiency" becomes "Boosted team efficiency by 35%, reducing project turnaround time from 6 weeks to 4 weeks and saving $75,000 annually"

v Balancing AI and Human Touch

- Importance of maintaining authenticity in AI-enhanced resumes
- Tips for customizing AI suggestions to reflect personal experiences

vi Future Trends in AI-Powered Job Search

- Predictive AI for career move suggestions
- Virtual Reality resumes for immersive skill showcasing
- AI-powered interview preparation tools

vii The New Resume Paradigm

- Shift from a list of jobs to a compelling narrative of professional journey
- AI as a powerful ally in crafting ATS-optimized and human-captivating resumes

This chapter sets the stage for a comprehensive exploration of AI's role in modern resume writing, promising to equip job seekers with cutting-edge tools and strategies for success in the competitive job market.

Module 1 - Quiz

1. **What is a resume referred to as in the context of the modern job market?**
    a. A detailed academic record.
    b. A digital handshake and first impression.
    c. A compilation of all past work experiences.
    d. A formal letter to hiring managers.

2. **Which AI tool is best for creating visually appealing resumes?**
    a. ChatGPT.
    b. Grammarly.
    c. Canva AI Resume Tools.
    d. LinkedIn Resume Builder.

3. **What is a significant challenge faced by job seekers in the modern job market?**
    a. Limited access to job postings.
    b. Recruiters spending only 6–8 seconds reviewing a resume.
    c. Lack of digital job boards.
    d. Inability to write resumes without AI tools.

4. **How can job seekers maintain authenticity in AI-enhanced resumes?**
    a. Fully rely on AI tools to craft the resume.
    b. Copy job descriptions directly into the resume.
    c. Customize AI-generated content and fact-check suggestions.
    d. Avoid using AI for resume writing entirely.

Answer Key

1. b. To act as a digital handshake and first impression
2. c. Canva AI Resume Tools
3. b. Recruiters spending only 6–8 seconds reviewing a resume
4. c. Customize AI-generated content and fact-check suggestions

PERSONAL SUMMARY
PERSONAL SUMMARY
PERSONAL SUMMARY

THE ROLE OF AI IN RESUME BUILDING

In today's competitive job market, artificial intelligence (AI) has revolutionized the process of resume creation, transforming it from a time-consuming task into a strategic tool for career advancement. This chapter explores the multifaceted role of AI in resume building, providing students with a comprehensive guide to leveraging AI tools effectively across various industries.

Understanding AI in Resume Building

AI-powered resume builders use advanced algorithms and natural language processing to analyze job descriptions, identify key skills and qualifications, and generate tailored content. These tools can significantly streamline the resume creation process, offering several advantages:

- **Efficiency and Time-Saving:** AI can generate a first draft of a resume in minutes, saving hours of manual work.
- **ATS Optimization:** AI tools ensure resumes are optimized for Applicant Tracking Systems (ATS) by incorporating relevant keywords and formatting.
- **Personalization:** AI can tailor resumes to specific industries or job roles, making applications more relevant and impactful.
- **Language Enhancement:** AI-powered grammar and style checkers improve the overall quality of writing.
- **Design and Formatting:** Some AI tools offer visually appealing templates and formatting suggestions.

Key AI Tools for Resume Building

- **ChatGPT:** This versatile AI can generate summaries, bullet points, and even entire resumes based on provided information. Use ChatGPT to generate a basic resume structure and content.
- **ResyMatch.io:** Specializes in ATS optimization by comparing resumes against job descriptions.
- **Canva:** Offers AI-powered design suggestions and industry-specific templates.
- **Grammarly:** Provides advanced grammar and style checking, as well as tone adjustment for professional communication.
- **SkillSyncer:** Matches resumes to job descriptions and highlights skills to emphasize. Ensures all relevant skills are used.
- **LinkedIn Resume Builder:** Generates resumes directly from LinkedIn profiles.

Industry-Specific AI Prompts

Here are AI prompts tailored for six common industries, with six prompts for each:

i   Technology

- "Create a resume summary for a full-stack developer with expertise in React, Node.js, and AWS."
- "Generate bullet points highlighting achievements in cybersecurity for a senior IT security analyst."
- "Write a skills section for a data scientist specializing in machine learning and big data analytics."
- "Craft experience descriptions for a project manager in an agile software development environment."

- "Develop a professional summary for a UX/UI designer with a focus on mobile app design."
- "Create bullet points showcasing cloud migration projects for a cloud solutions architect."

ii Healthcare

- "Write a resume summary for a registered nurse with experience in critical care and emergency medicine."
- "Generate bullet points highlighting patient care achievements for a primary care physician."
- "Craft a skills section for a healthcare administrator focusing on operational efficiency and regulatory compliance."
- "Develop experience descriptions for a medical researcher specializing in oncology clinical trials."
- "Create a professional summary for a physical therapist with expertise in sports rehabilitation."
- "Write bullet points showcasing telemedicine initiatives for a healthcare IT specialist."

iii Finance

- "Generate a resume summary for a financial analyst with expertise in mergers and acquisitions."
- "Create bullet points highlighting risk management achievements for a senior investment banker."
- "Craft a skills section for a quantitative trader specializing in algorithmic trading strategies."
- "Write experience descriptions for a corporate finance manager focusing on capital budgeting and financial forecasting."
- "Develop a professional summary for a certified public accountant with forensic accounting experience."
- "Generate bullet points showcasing fintech innovation projects for a digital banking product manager."

iv Marketing

- "Create a resume summary for a digital marketing manager specializing in SEO and content marketing."
- "Write bullet points highlighting social media campaign achievements for a brand strategist."
- "Craft a skills section for a marketing analytics specialist focusing on data-driven decision making."
- "Develop experience descriptions for an e-commerce marketing director emphasizing conversion rate optimization."
- "Generate a professional summary for a public relations specialist with crisis management expertise."
- "Create bullet points showcasing influencer marketing initiatives for a social media manager."

v Education

- "Write a resume summary for a high school science teacher with experience in STEM program development."
- "Generate bullet points highlighting student achievement improvements for an elementary school principal."
- "Craft a skills section for an educational technology specialist focusing on e-learning platform implementation."
- "Develop experience descriptions for a university professor specializing in online and hybrid course delivery."
- "Create a professional summary for a special education coordinator with expertise in individualized education programs."
- "Write bullet points showcasing curriculum development projects for an instructional designer."

vi Sales

- "Generate a resume summary for a B2B sales manager with a track record of exceeding revenue targets."

- "Create bullet points highlighting customer retention achievements for an account executive in SaaS sales."
- "Craft a skills section for a sales operations analyst focusing on CRM optimization and sales forecasting."
- "Write experience descriptions for a pharmaceutical sales representative emphasizing product launches and territory growth."
- "Develop a professional summary for a real estate broker specializing in luxury property sales."
- "Generate bullet points showcasing sales training and coaching initiatives for a sales enablement manager."

Best Practices for Using AI in Resume Building

- **Customize AI-generated content:** While AI can provide a solid foundation, it's crucial to personalize the content to reflect your unique experiences and voice.
- **Verify information:** Always double-check AI-generated content for accuracy and relevance to your specific situation.
- **Maintain authenticity:** Ensure your resume remains true to your experiences and skills, using AI as a tool for enhancement rather than fabrication.
- **Combine multiple AI tools:** Utilize different AI tools for various aspects of resume building to create a well-rounded document.
- **Keep human touch:** While AI can greatly assist in resume creation, the final review and personal touches should come from you.

Limitations and Ethical Considerations

While AI tools offer significant advantages, it's important to be aware of their limitations:

- Potential for generic content: Over-reliance on AI can lead to generic-sounding resumes.

- Lack of context understanding: AI may not fully grasp the nuances of your career trajectory or industry-specific jargon.
- Privacy concerns: Be cautious about sharing sensitive personal information with AI tools.

Ethically, it's crucial to use AI as a supportive tool rather than a replacement for your own input and honesty in resume creation.

Addressing Common Concerns

- Will employers know I used AI to write my resume?

AI-generated content, when properly customized, is indistinguishable from human-written text.

- How can I ensure my resume remains unique when using AI?

Personalize AI-generated content with your specific experiences and achievements.

- Are there any legal issues with using AI for resume writing?

Using AI tools for resume writing is legal, but ensure all information provided is truthful and accurate.

Conclusion

AI has become an invaluable asset in resume building, offering efficiency, optimization, and personalization. By understanding how to effectively use AI tools and prompts, students can create compelling, tailored resumes that stand out in today's competitive job market. Remember, while AI can significantly enhance the resume-building process, the most successful resumes will always incorporate personal insight, authenticity, and a human touch. For more in-depth tutorials and examples, students can refer to YouTube channels like "Resume Writing Academy" or "Career Vidz," which offer detailed guides on using AI for resume creation. Additionally, platforms like Coursera and edX offer courses on leveraging AI in job search strategies, providing comprehensive learning resources for students looking to master AI-assisted resume building.

Key Points from Chapter 2: The Role of AI in Resume Building

i   Revolutionizing Resume Creation

AI has transformed resume building from a tedious task into a strategic career tool by leveraging advanced algorithms and natural language processing.

ii   Advantages of AI in Resume Building

- **Efficiency:** Saves time by generating resumes quickly.
- **ATS Optimization:** Ensures resumes are optimized for Applicant Tracking Systems with relevant keywords.
- **Personalization:** Tailors content to specific roles and industries.
- **Language Enhancement:** Improves grammar and writing style.
- **Design and Formatting:** Offers professional templates and formatting suggestions.

iii   Key AI Tools for Resume Building

- **ChatGPT:** Generates summaries, bullet points, and complete resumes.
- **ResyMatch.io:** Optimizes resumes by aligning them with job descriptions.
- **Canva:** Provides visually appealing templates with design suggestions.
- **Grammarly:** Enhances grammar, tone, and professional writing style.
- **SkillSyncer:** Highlights and matches skills to job descriptions.
- **LinkedIn Resume Builder:** Extracts and formats resumes from LinkedIn profiles.

iv Industry-Specific AI Prompts

- **Technology:** Prompts for developers, cybersecurity experts, and project managers.
- **Healthcare:** Summaries and bullet points for nurses, physicians, and IT specialists.
- **Finance:** Content for financial analysts, traders, and CPAs.
- **Marketing:** Achievements for digital marketers, PR specialists, and strategists.
- **Education:** Tailored prompts for teachers, coordinators, and professors.
- **Sales:** Bullet points for managers, account executives, and real estate brokers.

v Best Practices for AI-Assisted Resume Building

- **Customization:** Personalize AI-generated content to reflect unique experiences.
- **Accuracy:** Verify the relevance and correctness of AI suggestions.
- **Authenticity:** Use AI for enhancement without fabricating information.
- **Combining Tools:** Leverage multiple tools for a comprehensive resume.
- **Human Touch:** Finalize resumes with a personal review and refinement.

vi Limitations and Ethical Considerations

- **Generic Output Risk:** Over-reliance can lead to generic resumes.
- **Lack of Context Understanding:** AI may not grasp industry nuances.
- **Privacy Concerns:** Avoid sharing sensitive data with AI tools.

- **Ethical Use:** Use AI as a supportive tool, ensuring honesty in content.

vii Addressing Common Concerns

- **Visibility:** Properly customized AI content is indistinguishable from human-written resumes.
- **Uniqueness:** Personalize AI content with specific achievements.
- **Legal Aspects:** AI use is legal, but accuracy and truthfulness are crucial.

viii Conclusion

- AI enhances resume creation with efficiency, personalization, and optimization.
- A successful resume blends AI insights with personal authenticity.
- For deeper understanding, students can explore tutorials on platforms like YouTube (e.g., "Resume Writing Academy") or take relevant courses on Coursera and edX.

Module 2 – Quiz

1. **What is a key advantage of AI in resume building?**
   a. Manual formatting of resumes.
   b. Tailoring resumes to specific job roles.
   c. Eliminating the need for job descriptions.
   d. Replacing the need for human oversight.

2. **Which AI tool specializes in ATS optimization?**
   a. Grammarly.
   b. Canva.
   c. ResyMatch.io.
   d. ChatGPT.

3. **What is a common limitation of AI in resume building?**
   a. Inability to use keywords.
   b. Over-reliance can lead to generic resumes.
   c. AI lacks the ability to generate formatted resumes.
   d. AI cannot assist in grammar improvement.

4. **What is recommended to maintain authenticity in an AI-assisted resume?**
   a. Avoid personalizing AI-generated content.
   b. Combine multiple AI tools for better results.
   c. Fully rely on AI without reviewing output.
   d. Use AI to fabricate achievements.

Answer Key

1. b. Tailoring resumes to specific job roles.
2. c. ResyMatch.io.
3. b. Over-reliance can lead to generic resumes.
4. b. Combine multiple AI tools for better results.

ATS AND KEYEHVEGES
STRATEGI S
OP Resume Opimzation
ATS
RESUMES
KHBHWROS
SEASLALE
HUMAN-AI
OLALIBATION
ATS ad Keew
Resume Op
Heshold Keehner
Highted Keywoo
AI

ATS AND KEYWORD STRATEGIES FOR RESUME OPTIMIZATION

In today's competitive job market, understanding how to navigate Applicant Tracking Systems (ATS) and optimize resumes for keyword relevance is crucial for job seekers. This module provides in-depth insights into ATS, the importance of keywords, and strategies to effectively use them in your resume.

Understanding ATS and the Role of Keywords

Applicant Tracking Systems (ATS) are sophisticated software tools used by companies to screen, sort, and manage job applications. These systems scan resumes for specific keywords and phrases related to the job description, helping employers filter through large volumes of applications efficiently. Keywords are the lifeblood of getting your resume past the ATS gatekeepers. They act as a bridge between your professional experience and the specific requirements of a job description. When your resume contains the right keywords, it has a better chance of passing through the ATS and reaching human reviewers.

The Importance of Keywords

Using the right keywords in your resume is crucial for several reasons:

- ATS Compatibility: Many companies use ATS to screen resumes before they reach human eyes. If your resume doesn't contain the right keywords, it may be automatically rejected.

- Relevance Demonstration: Keywords help you demonstrate that you possess the skills and experience necessary for the job.
- Increased Visibility: When employers use keywords to search their database of resumes, those containing relevant keywords are more likely to appear in search results.
- Time Efficiency: Keywords help employers quickly identify candidates who match their criteria, saving time in the recruitment process.

ATS Keywords for Different Industries

Here are examples of ATS keywords for six different industries:

i   Information Technology:
- Programming languages (e.g., Python, Java, C++)
- Cloud computing (e.g., AWS, Azure)
- Cybersecurity
- Machine learning
- Agile methodology

ii   Healthcare:
- Patient care
- Electronic Health Records (EHR)
- HIPAA compliance
- Clinical trials
- Medical coding

iii Finance:
- Financial analysis
- Risk management
- Investment strategies

- Regulatory compliance
- Financial modeling

iv Marketing:

- Digital marketing
- SEO/SEM
- Content strategy
- Social media management
- Analytics

v Education:

- Curriculum development
- Student assessment
- Classroom management
- E-learning platforms
- Special education

vi Human Resources:

- Talent acquisition
- Employee relations
- Performance management
- HRIS systems
- Diversity and inclusion

Consequences of Not Using Keywords

Failing to use appropriate keywords in your resume can have several negative outcomes:

- ATS Rejection: Your resume may be filtered out by the ATS before it reaches a human reviewer.
- Missed Opportunities: Employers searching resume databases using specific keywords may not find your application.

- Perceived Lack of Relevance: Without relevant keywords, your resume may appear less aligned with the job requirements, even if you're well-qualified.
- Wasted Effort: Submitting resumes without proper keyword optimization can result in a lot of applications with little to no response.

Disadvantages of Overusing Keywords

While keywords are important, overusing them can have negative consequences:

- Keyword Stuffing: Excessive use of keywords can make your resume appear unnatural and may be flagged by ATS as an attempt to game the system
- Reduced Readability: Overloading your resume with keywords can make it difficult for human readers to understand your actual qualifications and experiences.
- Loss of Authenticity: Focusing too much on keywords may lead to a generic resume that doesn't effectively showcase your unique skills and experiences.
- Potential for Misrepresentation: Using keywords that don't accurately reflect your skills or experience can lead to uncomfortable situations in interviews.

Free AI Tools for Generating ATS Keywords

Several free AI-powered tools can help you generate relevant ATS keywords for job descriptions:

- Jobscan: Compares resume to job descriptions and offers limited free scans.
- ResyMatch: Free tool for optimizing ATS keyword relevance.
- Zety: Helps generate industry-specific keywords.
- SkillSyncer: Generates industry-specific keywords with a free basic version.

- LinkedIn Skills Assessments: While not a direct keyword tool, it can help you identify relevant skills for your industry.

Prompts for Specific Industries

When using AI tools to generate keywords for specific industries, consider using prompts like these:
- "Generate relevant ATS keywords for a [job title] position in the [specific industry] sector."
- "What are the most important skills and qualifications for a [job title] in [industry]?"
- "List the top 10 technical terms used in job descriptions for [job title] in [industry]."
- "What certifications or qualifications are commonly required for [job title] roles in [industry]?"
- "Identify emerging trends and associated keywords in the [industry] field for [job title] positions."

How and Where to Use ATS Keywords in a Resume

To effectively incorporate ATS keywords in your resume:
Professional Summary: Include relevant keywords in your professional summary or objective statement at the top of your resume.
Skills Section: Create a dedicated skills section that lists relevant technical skills, soft skills, and industry-specific keywords.
Work Experience: Incorporate keywords naturally into your job descriptions and achievements.
- Education and Certifications: Include relevant degrees, certifications, and training programs that match the job requirements.
- Projects or Additional Sections: If applicable, create sections for projects, publications, or volunteer work that allow you to showcase additional relevant keywords.

Remember to use keywords in context and ensure they accurately reflect your skills and experiences. Avoid keyword stuffing and maintain a natural, readable flow in your resume

Conclusion

Optimizing your resume for ATS and using relevant keywords is essential in today's job market. By understanding the role of ATS, identifying appropriate keywords for your industry, and strategically incorporating them into your resume, you can significantly increase your chances of getting past initial screenings and landing interviews. However, it's crucial to strike a balance between keyword optimization and maintaining a compelling, authentic representation of your skills and experiences. Use AI tools and industry-specific prompts to identify relevant keywords, but always ensure that your resume remains readable and genuinely reflects your qualifications. Remember, while ATS optimization is important, your ultimate goal is to impress human recruiters and hiring managers. A well-crafted, keyword-optimized resume that clearly communicates your value proposition will give you the best chance of success in your job search.

Key Points from Chapter 3: ATS and Keyword Strategies for Resume Optimization

i Understanding ATS and Keywords

- **What is ATS?** Applicant Tracking Systems (ATS) are software tools that screen and sort resumes for specific keywords, streamlining the recruitment process.
- **Role of Keywords:** Keywords connect your skills and experiences to job requirements, increasing the likelihood of passing ATS screening and reaching human recruiters.

ii Importance of Keywords in Resumes

- **ATS Compatibility:** Ensures your resume isn't rejected by ATS due to missing relevant keywords.
- **Relevance Demonstration:** Highlights your alignment with the job's requirements.
- **Increased Visibility:** Positions your resume higher in keyword-based searches by recruiters.
- **Time Efficiency for Employers:** Helps recruiters quickly identify suitable candidates.

iii Examples of ATS Keywords by Industry

- **IT:** Programming languages (e.g., Python), cloud computing, cybersecurity, agile methodology.
- **Healthcare:** Patient care, EHR, HIPAA compliance, clinical trials, medical coding.
- **Finance:** Financial analysis, risk management, investment strategies, regulatory compliance.
- **Marketing:** SEO, digital marketing, content strategy, social media management.
- **Education:** Curriculum development, e-learning platforms, student assessment, special education.
- **HR:** Talent acquisition, HRIS systems, diversity and inclusion, performance management.

iv   Consequences of Not Using Keywords

- **ATS Rejection:** Resumes without proper keywords may not reach human reviewers.
- **Missed Opportunities:** Employers may overlook resumes lacking relevant keywords during searches.
- **Perceived Irrelevance:** Your qualifications may appear disconnected from job requirements.
- **Inefficiency:** Submitting unoptimized resumes can result in fewer responses despite effort.

v   Disadvantages of Overusing Keywords

- **Keyword Stuffing:** Excessive keywords may trigger ATS red flags or reduce readability.
- **Reduced Readability:** Overloading resumes with keywords can obscure your actual qualifications.
- **Loss of Authenticity:** Overemphasis on keywords may result in a generic and impersonal resume.
- **Risk of Misrepresentation:** Including irrelevant or exaggerated keywords can lead to credibility issues in interviews.

vi   Free AI Tools for Generating ATS Keywords

- **Jobscan:** Limited free scans for resume and job description comparison.
- **ResyMatch.io:** Offers keyword optimization for ATS.
- **Zety:** Generates industry-specific keywords.
- **SkillSyncer:** Matches skills to job descriptions.
- **LinkedIn Skills Assessments:** Identifies relevant industry-specific skills.

vii   Prompts for Generating ATS Keywords

- "Generate relevant ATS keywords for [job title] in [specific industry]."

- "List essential qualifications for a [job title] in [industry]."
- "Identify emerging trends and related keywords for [industry]."

viii Strategic Placement of Keywords in Resumes

- **Professional Summary:** Integrate role-specific keywords to highlight alignment.
- **Skills Section:** List relevant technical and soft skills prominently.
- **Work Experience:** Embed keywords naturally into job descriptions and achievements.
- **Education and Certifications:** Highlight degrees and certifications relevant to the role.
- **Additional Sections:** Use project, publication, or volunteer work sections to add context for extra keywords.

ix Best Practices for ATS Keyword Usage

- **Contextual Integration:** Place keywords where they align naturally with your experience.
- **Avoid Keyword Stuffing:** Maintain readability and authenticity.
- **Verify Accuracy:** Ensure all keywords reflect your true skills and qualifications.

x Conclusion

- **Keyword Optimization is Crucial:** Strategically using relevant keywords can improve your chances of passing ATS screenings.
- **Balance is Key:** Combine keyword relevance with an authentic, compelling representation of your skills.
- **Leverage AI:** Use AI tools and industry-specific prompts to refine keyword strategies while maintaining a personal touch.
- **Goal:** Impress not only ATS but also human recruiters, ensuring your resume is both optimized and impactful.

Module 3 – Quiz

1. **What is the primary role of an Applicant Tracking System (ATS)?**
   a. To manually review resumes for formatting errors.
   b. To screen, sort, and manage job applications.
   c. To schedule interviews with candidates.
   d. To rank companies based on job postings.

2. **Which of the following is a common consequence of not using ATS keywords?**
   a. Improved readability of the resume.
   b. Higher chances of getting interview calls.
   c. ATS rejection before human review.
   d. Reduced need for resume formatting.

3. **What is a disadvantage of overusing keywords in a resume?**
   a. ATS rejection for lack of keywords.
   b. Loss of authenticity and natural flow.
   c. Enhanced understanding of qualifications by recruiters.
   d. Easier identification of skills by employers.

4. **Where is it most effective to incorporate ATS keywords in a resume?**
   a. In a separate cover letter only.
   b. Professional summary, skills, and work experience sections.
   c. Only in the education section.
   d. At the bottom of the resume for emphasis.

Answer Key

1. b. To screen, sort, and manage job applications.
2. c. ATS rejection before human review.
3. b. Loss of authenticity and natural flow.
4. b. Professional summary, skills, and work experience sections.

PERSONAL SUMMARY
PERSONAL SUMMARY

CRAFTING A PERSONAL SUMMARY

A personal summary, also known as a professional summary or resume summary statement, is a crucial component of your resume that provides a concise overview of your experience, skills, and qualifications. Positioned at the top of your resume, it serves as your introduction to potential employers and can significantly impact their first impression.

Importance of a Personal Summary

- First Impression: Captures the hiring manager's attention quickly.
- Time Efficiency: Conveys relevance quickly, as recruiters spend only 6-8 seconds on average reviewing a resume.
- ATS Compatibility: Helps your resume pass through Applicant Tracking Systems (ATS).
- Personal Branding: Showcases your unique strengths and professional identity.
- Strategic Positioning: Highlights your key qualifications to encourage further review of your resume.

Key Rules for Crafting an Effective Personal Summary

- Keep it concise: Aim for 3-5 sentences or 70-75 words.
- Tailor it to the specific job: Customize your summary for each application.
- Use strong action verbs and industry-specific keywords.
- Quantify achievements when possible.

- Focus on what you can offer the employer, not what you want from the job.
- Maintain a professional tone: Avoid personal pronouns like "I".

Incorporating ATS Keywords and Job Description

To optimize your personal summary for ATS:
- Analyze the job description for key skills and qualifications.
- Incorporate relevant keywords naturally into your summary.
- Use industry-specific terminology that matches the job listing.
- Ensure your summary aligns with the required experience level and job responsibilities.

Leveraging Past Experience

When crafting your summary:
- Highlight your most relevant accomplishments and skills.
- Use specific examples that demonstrate your expertise.
- Focus on experiences that directly relate to the job you're applying for.
- Showcase your unique selling points that set you apart from other candidates.

Steps to Align Your Personal Summary with the Job Description

- Carefully read the job description and highlight key requirements.
- Identify the most important skills and qualifications sought by the employer.
- Match your experiences and achievements to these requirements.
- Use similar language and terminology found in the job posting.

- Prioritize the most relevant information based on the job's priorities.
- Create a draft combining job requirements and your qualifications.
- Edit for clarity and professionalism.

Common Mistakes to Avoid

- Using generic statements that could apply to any candidate.
- Including irrelevant information or personal details.
- Writing in the first person (e.g., "I am a...").
- Making it too long or wordy.
- Overusing buzzwords without substantiating them with concrete examples.
- Keyword stuffing, which makes the summary unreadable and unprofessional.
- Ignoring the job description, resulting in a one-size-fits-all summary.

Best Platforms for Crafting Personal Summaries

- ChatGPT: Best for detailed summaries tailored to specific roles.
- Claude (Anthropic): Ideal for drafting concise summaries with excellent language quality.
- Perplexity: Suitable for research-backed summaries for niche industries.
- Other tools: Zety, Resume.io (ATS-ready templates), ResyMatch (ATS compliance), LinkedIn Profile Insights (industry-specific ideas).

How to Sell Yourself in Your Personal Summary

- **Use strong, confident language that highlights your expertise.**

Example: "Accomplished marketing professional with over 8 years of experience in developing data-driven campaigns that consistently exceed ROI targets by 30%."

Explanation: This statement uses confident language ("accomplished") and directly communicates expertise in a measurable way.

- **Focus on your unique selling points and what sets you apart from other candidates.**

Example: "Specialized in implementing innovative training programs that have increased employee productivity by 25%, setting my team apart as the top-performing division in the company."

Explanation: The emphasis is on a unique skill—innovative training—and how it contributes to organizational success, making the candidate stand out.

- **Quantify your achievements with specific metrics or results.**

Example: "Increased annual sales revenue by $2 million through strategic client acquisition and retention initiatives, achieving a 40% growth rate year-over-year."

Explanation: Including numbers (e.g., "$2 million," "40% growth") makes achievements tangible and demonstrates measurable impact.

- **Demonstrate how your skills and experience can benefit the employer.**

Example: "Leveraged advanced data analytics to reduce operational costs by 15%, directly aligning with the company's goal of driving cost efficiency."

Explanation: This ties the candidate's skills to solving a problem or meeting a goal relevant to the employer.

- **Show enthusiasm for the role and industry.**

Example: "Passionate about leveraging digital transformation strategies to revolutionize customer experiences within the retail sector."

Explanation: Expressing enthusiasm shows genuine interest in both the role and industry, which can resonate with hiring managers.

- **Highlight value you bring, such as increased efficiency or cost savings.**

Example: "Streamlined internal workflows, reducing project turnaround times by 20% and saving the company $50,000 annually."

Explanation: The candidate clearly articulates how their actions resulted in concrete benefits like time savings and cost reductions.

- **Mention specialized skills or certifications that set you apart.**

Example: *"Certified Project Management Professional (PMP) with expertise in Agile methodologies, leading cross-functional teams to deliver projects on time and under budget."*

Explanation: Highlighting certifications (e.g., PMP) and specialized knowledge (e.g., Agile) demonstrates qualifications that differentiate the candidate from others.

Where to Use the Personal Summary

- Resume: As the opening section to draw the recruiter's attention.
- LinkedIn Profile: As the "About" section to enhance online visibility.
- Job Portals: Tailor summaries for ATS-focused platforms like Indeed or Monster.
- Cover Letters: Adapt it into a compelling opening paragraph.

Best AI Prompts for Industry-Specific Personal Summaries

When using AI tools to generate industry-specific personal summaries, consider these prompts:

- **Information Technology:**

"Generate a concise personal summary for a senior software developer with 10 years of experience in cloud computing and machine learning. Include key programming languages and highlight achievements in improving system efficiency."

- **Healthcare:**

"Create a personal summary for a registered nurse specializing in pediatric care with 5 years of experience. Emphasize patient care skills, knowledge of electronic health records, and any certifications."

- **Finance:**

"Craft a personal summary for a financial analyst with expertise in risk management and investment strategies. Highlight quantifiable achievements and knowledge of regulatory compliance."

- **Marketing:**

"Develop a personal summary for a digital marketing manager with experience in SEO, content strategy, and social media campaigns. Include metrics on campaign success and expertise with marketing analytics tools."

- **Education:**

"Generate a personal summary for a high school science teacher with 8 years of experience. Focus on curriculum development skills, use of e-learning platforms, and success in improving student engagement and test scores."

- **Human Resources:**

"Create a personal summary for an HR manager specializing in talent acquisition and employee relations. Highlight experience with HRIS systems and achievements in improving retention rates and implementing diversity initiatives."

Human Intervention in AI-Generated Summaries

While AI tools can provide a solid foundation for your personal summary, human intervention is crucial for creating a truly effective and personalized statement. Here's how and where human input is needed:

- Customization: After generating the AI summary, review and customize it to reflect your unique voice and experiences. This typically requires 15-20 minutes of editing.

- Accuracy Check: Ensure all information is accurate and truly reflects your experience. This may take 5-10 minutes.
- Keyword Integration: While AI can include relevant keywords, you should spend 10-15 minutes fine-tuning keyword placement to ensure they flow naturally and align with the specific job description.
- Tone Adjustment: Adjust the tone to match the company culture and industry norms. This might require 10-15 minutes of refinement.
- Quantification: Add specific, quantifiable achievements that the AI might not have included. This could take 15-20 minutes of reflection and writing.
- Final Polish: Spend 10-15 minutes on a final review, ensuring the summary is concise, impactful, and free of errors.

In total, expect to spend 60-90 minutes refining an AI-generated summary to create a truly personalized and effective statement.

Conclusion

Crafting an effective personal summary is crucial for creating a compelling resume. By tailoring your summary to the specific job, incorporating relevant keywords, and highlighting your most impressive qualifications, you can significantly increase your chances of catching a hiring manager's attention. While AI tools can be helpful in generating ideas and providing a starting point, the most effective summaries will always be those that genuinely reflect your individual experiences and voice. Remember to keep it concise, focused, and aligned with the job description. With practice, refinement, and the strategic use of AI-assisted tools, your personal summary can become a powerful asset in your job search, opening doors to new opportunities and setting you apart from the competition.

Key Points from Chapter 4: Crafting a Personal Summary

i Definition and Importance of a Personal Summary

- A personal summary is a concise overview of your experience, skills, and qualifications, positioned at the top of your resume.
- It serves as an introduction, creating a strong first impression for hiring managers and optimizing resumes for ATS.
- Benefits include showcasing personal branding, conveying relevance, and highlighting unique strengths.

ii Key Rules for Writing an Effective Personal Summary

- **Concise:** Limit to 3-5 sentences or 70-75 words.
- **Tailored:** Customize for each job application.
- **Impactful:** Use strong action verbs, keywords, and quantifiable achievements.
- **Professional:** Avoid personal pronouns like "I" and maintain a formal tone.
- **Employer-Focused:** Emphasize value to the employer, not personal aspirations.

iii Optimizing for ATS

- Extract relevant skills and qualifications from the job description.
- Incorporate industry-specific terminology naturally.
- Align the summary with the job's required experience and responsibilities.

iv Leveraging Past Experience

- Highlight relevant accomplishments and unique selling points.
- Use specific examples that demonstrate expertise.

- Showcase achievements that directly relate to the job requirements.

v   Steps to Align Your Summary with the Job Description

- Analyze the job description and identify key requirements.
- Match experiences and skills to these requirements using job-specific language.
- Draft and refine for clarity and professionalism, prioritizing relevant details.

vi   Common Mistakes to Avoid

- Using generic, one-size-fits-all statements.
- Including irrelevant details or personal pronouns.
- Overusing buzzwords or stuffing keywords unnaturally.
- Writing overly lengthy summaries.
- Ignoring the job description, resulting in a misaligned summary.

vii   Platforms and AI Tools for Crafting Personal Summaries

- **ChatGPT:** Detailed, tailored summaries for specific roles.
- **Claude:** Concise summaries with professional language quality.
- **ResyMatch.io and Zety:** ATS-ready templates and keyword suggestions.
- **LinkedIn Profile Insights:** Industry-specific ideas for summaries.

viii   How to Sell Yourself in a Personal Summary

- Use confident language and quantify achievements with specific metrics.
- Focus on unique skills and contributions relevant to the employer.
- Demonstrate enthusiasm for the role and industry.

- Highlight certifications or specialized expertise that sets you apart.
- Showcase value through measurable results, such as increased efficiency or cost savings.

ix Where to Use a Personal Summary

- Resume: As the opening section.
- LinkedIn Profile: "About" section to enhance visibility.
- Job Portals: Tailor for ATS-driven platforms.
- Cover Letters: Adapt as an engaging opening paragraph.

x Human Intervention in AI-Generated Summaries

- **Customization:** Edit for personal voice and accuracy (15-20 minutes).
- **Keyword Integration:** Refine placement for natural flow (10-15 minutes).
- **Quantification:** Add measurable achievements (15-20 minutes).
- **Final Polish:** Review for conciseness and impact (10-15 minutes).

xi Conclusion

- A well-crafted personal summary is critical for capturing attention and showcasing your qualifications.
- Balance ATS optimization with a genuine representation of your skills and experiences.
- Use AI tools to draft summaries but invest time in personalizing and refining them.
- By keeping your summary concise, relevant, and impactful, you can create a compelling introduction that sets you apart in a competitive job market.

Module 4 – Quiz

1. **What is the primary purpose of a personal summary?**
   a. To list all work experience in detail.
   b. To provide a concise overview of skills and qualifications.
   c. To replace the need for a cover letter.
   d. To showcase academic achievements exclusively.

2. **Which is a key rule for crafting an effective personal summary?**
   a. Use personal pronouns like "I."
   b. Focus on what you want from the job.
   c. Quantify achievements when possible.
   d. Write generic statements applicable to any job.

3. **What is a common mistake to avoid in a personal summary?**
   a. Using industry-specific keywords.
   b. Including irrelevant personal details.
   c. Tailoring the summary for specific jobs.
   d. Highlighting measurable achievements.

4. **Where can a personal summary be effectively used?**
   a. Only on printed resumes.
   b. As the "About" section on LinkedIn.
   c. Exclusively in cover letters.
   d. At the bottom of a resume.

Answer Key

1. b. To provide a concise overview of skills and qualifications.
2. c. Quantify achievements when possible.
3. b. Including irrelevant personal details.
4. b. As the "About" section on LinkedIn.

SKILL MAPPING
SKILL MAPPING

SKILL MAPPING AND HIGHLIGHTING – THE ART OF SHOWCASING YOUR EXPERTISE

In this chapter, we'll explore the crucial role of skills in resume writing and how to effectively present them to stand out in the job market.

Why Skills Matter

Skills are the backbone of your professional profile. They showcase your capabilities and demonstrate your value to potential employers. By highlighting the right skills, you increase your chances of passing through Applicant Tracking Systems (ATS) and catching the eye of recruiters. For instance, a Project Manager highlighting skills like "Budget management" and "Risk analysis" immediately signals their expertise in critical areas.

Identifying ATS-Compliant Skills

To make your resume ATS-compliant, focus on extracting keywords from job descriptions. Use tools like SkillSyncer, ResumeUp.AI, or Jobscan to scan job postings and identify relevant skills. Remember, ATS systems look for exact matches, so use the same terminology as the job description. For example, if the job posting mentions "data analysis," use that exact phrase rather than "analyzing data."

Locating Skills in Job Descriptions

Skills are typically found in these sections of job descriptions:

- Key Responsibilities: Often list hard skills, e.g., "Data analysis"
- Preferred/Desired Skills: Contain soft skills, e.g., "Team leadership"
- Requirements: Here you'll find certifications, technical skills, and must-haves

Pay attention to both technical (hard) and interpersonal (soft) skills mentioned throughout the posting.

Creating a Generic Resume

For an all-purpose resume, include a mix of technical and transferable skills. Some universally valuable skills are:

- Communication
- Problem-solving
- Teamwork
- Time management
- Adaptability
- Leadership
- Technical proficiency (relevant to your field)
- Microsoft Office
- Project management tools (e.g., Jira, Trello)

These skills appeal broadly but may lack specificity for ATS. Always tailor your resume for specific job applications when possible.

Job-Specific Skills and AI Prompts

Here are some common jobs with important skills and AI prompts to use:

- **Software Developer**

Skills: Java, Python, SQL, Agile methodologies, Git, Debugging, API Development

Prompt: "List top 10 in-demand skills for a software developer in 2024, focusing on backend development"

- **Marketing Manager**

Skills: SEO, content strategy, social media management, data analysis, PPC, campaign management

Prompt: "What are the essential skills for a digital marketing manager with an SEO focus?"

- **Financial Analyst**

Skills: Financial modeling, Excel, SQL, risk analysis, forecasting, budgeting, data visualization

Prompt: "Generate key skills for a financial analyst position in banking"

- **Project Manager**

Skills: Agile, Scrum, budgeting, risk management, stakeholder communication

Prompt: "What skills should a project manager highlight on their resume for tech companies?"

- **Data Scientist**

Skills: Python, R, machine learning, statistical analysis, data visualization

Prompt: "List crucial skills for a data scientist role in 2024"

- **Human Resources Manager**

Skills: Recruitment, employee relations, performance management, HRIS, talent acquisition, training, onboarding

Prompt: "What are the top skills for an HR manager focusing on L&D and talent management?"

Finding Skills on LinkedIn

On LinkedIn job postings, look for the "Skills Match" section at the top of the job description. This shows the key skills required for the role and how well your profile matches. Additionally, analyze endorsements and top skills on profiles of people in similar roles. For example, for a Learning & Development Specialist, LinkedIn may highlight "Instructional design" and "LMS management."

Free AI Tools for ATS Skills

Some free AI tools to extract ATS-friendly skills include:
- SkillSyncer
- ResumeUp.AI
- Jobscan (limited free scans)
- RezRunner
- ResyMatch.io

Balancing AI and Human Touch

While AI tools are helpful, don't rely on them entirely. Use AI to:
- Extract skills from job descriptions
- Refine wording
- Check ATS compatibility

Always review and customize the results to match your unique experience and the specific job requirements. Your personal touch and judgment are crucial in creating a compelling resume.

Checking Skill Match Percentage

Some ATS and resume optimization tools provide a percentage match between your resume and the job description. Aim for at least a 70-80% match for better chances of passing the initial screening. Tools like Jobscan can help you analyze your resume against the job description.

Ideal Length for Skills Section

Keep your skills section concise, typically 8-12 key skills. For technical roles, you might include more. Skills should be 1–3 words to ensure clarity. Avoid long phrases. For example, instead of "Ability to manage cross-functional teams," use "Cross-functional collaboration."

Placement of Skills on Resume

Place your skills section prominently, usually after your professional summary and before your work experience. This allows recruiters to quickly assess your qualifications. However, don't limit skills to just one section:

- Skills Section: A dedicated section for quick scanning
- Personal Summary: Incorporate relevant skills naturally
- Roles and Responsibilities: Mention specific skills tied to achievements

Incorporating Skills in Summary and Roles

Weave relevant skills into your professional summary and job descriptions. For example:

Summary: "Results-driven marketing manager with expertise in SEO and content strategy..."

Role: "Led a team of 5, utilizing Agile methodologies to deliver projects 15% ahead of schedule." In your roles, show how skills drive results. For instance: "Implemented LMS system, increasing training completion rates by 25%."

Importance of Skill Integration

Yes, it's crucial to incorporate skills mentioned in your summary and roles throughout your resume. This reinforces your proficiency and helps with ATS keyword matching. Repetition (within reason) can emphasize your key strengths.

Tailoring Skills for Each Application

It's best to tailor your skills for each job application. This ensures you're highlighting the most relevant abilities for each position and improves your chances of passing ATS screenings. For example, a generic resume might use "Project management," while a specific role could require "Agile project management." Remember, your resume is a dynamic document. Keep refining and updating your skills as you grow professionally and as job requirements evolve. By mastering the art of skill mapping and highlighting, you'll create a resume that not only passes ATS checks but also impresses human recruiters, bringing you one step closer to landing your dream job.

Key Points from Chapter 5: Skill Mapping and Highlighting – The Art of Showcasing Your Expertise

i Why Skills Matter in Resumes

- Skills are a cornerstone of your professional profile, showcasing your expertise and value to employers.
- Highlighting relevant skills improves ATS compatibility and attracts recruiters' attention.
- Example: A Project Manager highlighting "Budget management" signals expertise in critical areas.

ii Identifying ATS-Compliant Skills

- Use tools like **SkillSyncer**, **ResumeUp.AI**, and **Jobscan** to extract keywords from job descriptions.
- Match exact phrases (e.g., "Data analysis" instead of "Analyzing data") to optimize ATS compatibility.

iii Locating Skills in Job Descriptions

- **Key Responsibilities:** Contain hard skills (e.g., "Data visualization").
- **Preferred Skills:** Focus on soft skills (e.g., "Team leadership").
- **Requirements:** Include certifications, technical skills, and must-haves.

iv Generic vs. Tailored Resumes

- A **generic resume** should include transferable skills like communication, problem-solving, and adaptability.
- For specific roles, tailor skills to align with the job description for better ATS performance.

v   Industry-Specific Skills and AI Prompts

- **Software Developer:** Java, Python, Agile methodologies.
- **Marketing Manager:** SEO, social media management, campaign strategy.
- **Financial Analyst:** Forecasting, risk analysis, financial modeling.
- Use AI prompts like: "What are the top 10 skills for [job title] in [industry]?"

vi   Leveraging LinkedIn for Skill Insights

- Analyze the **Skills Match** section in job postings.
- Review endorsed skills on profiles of professionals in similar roles.

vii   Free AI Tools for Skill Identification

- Tools like **RezRunner**, **ResyMatch.io**, and **Jobscan** help extract ATS-friendly skills.
- Balance AI suggestions with human judgment for customization and authenticity.

viii   Ideal Length and Placement of Skills Section

- Keep the skills section concise, listing 8-12 key skills (1-3 words each).
- Place prominently after the professional summary for quick recruiter review.
- Incorporate skills in **roles and responsibilities** to demonstrate their practical application.

ix   Tailoring Skills for Job Applications

- Use dynamic tailoring to align your skills with each job description.
- Example: Use "Agile project management" instead of "Project management" if the job specifies Agile expertise.

x   Integrating Skills Throughout the Resume

- **Skills Section:** Highlight key qualifications.
- **Professional Summary:** Include skills naturally in the context of your expertise.
- **Work Experience:** Demonstrate how skills contributed to measurable achievements.
- Example: "Led Agile projects, reducing delivery time by 20%."

xi   Checking Skill Match Percentage

- Use tools like **Jobscan** to aim for a 70-80% match with job descriptions, enhancing ATS success.

xii   Balancing AI and Human Touch

- AI can extract and refine skills, but human intervention ensures relevance, accuracy, and personalization.
- Use AI as a starting point and invest time in tailoring skills for impact.

xiii Conclusion

- Effective skill mapping transforms your resume into a targeted and impactful document.
- Highlighting the right skills increases ATS compatibility and impresses recruiters.
- Tailor your skills for each application, integrate them throughout your resume, and balance AI insights with personal customization for maximum effectiveness.

Module 5 – Quiz

1. **Why are skills crucial in resumes?**
    a. They replace the need for work experience.
    b. They demonstrate value and improve ATS compatibility.
    c. They reduce the time needed to write a resume.
    d. They are the only component recruiters care about.

2. **What is the best way to identify ATS-compliant skills?**
    a. Use vague terms that apply to any job.
    b. Rely solely on past experience without analyzing job descriptions.
    c. Extract keywords directly from job descriptions.
    d. Avoid using tools like Jobscan or SkillSyncer.

3. **What is the ideal length for a skills section?**
    a. 3-5 skills, with long descriptions.
    b. 8-12 concise skills, each 1-3 words long.
    c. 15-20 skills in detailed paragraphs.
    d. As many skills as possible, regardless of formatting.

4. **Where should skills be placed on a resume for maximum impact?**
    a. At the bottom of the resume.
    b. In a cover letter instead of the resume.
    c. After the professional summary and integrated into roles.
    d. Only in the work experience section.

Answer Key

1. b. They demonstrate value and improve ATS compatibility.
2. c. Extract keywords directly from job descriptions.
3. b. 8-12 concise skills, each 1-3 words long.
4. c. After the professional summary and integrated into roles.

SUCCESS
AMEGREMENTS
SUCCESS
ACHIVEMENTS
ACHIVEMENTS
SUCCESS
ACHIMENTS
33%
SUCCESS
SUCCEST
ACHIMENT

SHOWCASING ACHIEVEMENTS – CRAFTING YOUR PROFESSIONAL SUCCESS STORY

The Power of Accomplishments: Why Achievements Matter

Achievements are the compelling highlights that capture a recruiter's attention. They offer tangible proof of your capabilities and potential, providing a snapshot of past successes that can predict future performance. Including achievements in your resume is crucial for:

- Differentiation: Standing out in a sea of job seekers
- Value Proposition: Communicating your unique contributions
- Evidence of Success: Providing concrete proof of competence
- Credibility: Adding weight to your experience through quantifiable results
- Storytelling: Narrating your problem-solving and innovation journey

The Art of Humble Leadership: Showcasing Without Bragging

Striking a balance between confidence and humility is key. Here's how to do it:

- Use action verbs: Start with words like "Led," "Implemented," or "Developed"
- Focus on results: Emphasize outcomes rather than just your role
- Quantify where possible: Use numbers to provide concrete evidence
- Use "we" for team efforts: Show you're a team player while highlighting your contribution

Example: "Led a cross-functional team that increased sales by 30% over six months" instead of "I single-handedly boosted sales."

Strategic Placement: Where to Showcase Your Wins

Incorporate achievements throughout your resume:
- Professional Summary: Highlight your most impressive accomplishments
- Work Experience: Include 3-5 key achievements for each relevant role
- Skills Section: Tie specific skills to measurable achievements
- Projects or Additional Sections: For freelancers or those with notable side projects

The Achievement Formula: STAR and CAR Techniques

Use the Situation-Task-Action-Result (STAR) or Context-Action-Result (CAR) techniques to structure your achievements:
- Situation/Context: Describe the challenge or situation you faced
- Task: Explain what you were tasked with (for STAR)
- Action: Detail what you did to address the challenge
- Result: Highlight the outcome of your actions, preferably with quantifiable metrics

Example using CAR: "Implemented a new inventory management system (Action) for a rapidly growing e-commerce startup (Context), resulting in a 25% reduction in stockouts and a 15% increase in order fulfillment speed (Result)."

ATS-Friendly Achievements: Passing the Digital Gatekeeper

Ensure your achievements are ATS-compliant:
- Use clear, standard job titles
- Incorporate relevant keywords from the job description
- Avoid complex formatting or graphics
- Use a simple, clean layout that's easy for both ATS and human readers to parse

Example: If the job description emphasizes "cost savings," write: "Reduced operational expenses by 20% through process optimization."

Fresh Starts and New Beginnings: Achievements for Freshers and Career Transitioners

Even without extensive work experience, you can showcase achievements:
- Academic projects: Highlight successful group projects or individual research
- Volunteer work: Emphasize leadership roles or measurable community impacts
- Internships or part-time jobs: Focus on improvements or efficiencies you brought
- Personal projects: Showcase relevant skills through side projects or hobbies

Example: "Developed a budgeting app as a personal project, gaining 1000+ users within three months."

Industry Spotlights: Achievement Examples Across Sectors

Here are examples of achievements across six different industries:

i   Software Engineering

- Developed an algorithm that improved data processing speed by 40%
- Contributed to open-source projects with over 100,000 downloads
- Cut down security breaches by 97% for clients

ii   Marketing

- Increased social media engagement by 75% through targeted content strategy
- Led a rebranding campaign that resulted in a 25% increase in brand recognition
- Developed an email marketing campaign with a 35% higher open rate than industry average

iii   Finance

- Implemented cost-saving measures that reduced operational expenses by 15%
- Managed a portfolio that outperformed market indices by 10% over two years
- Analyzed 3 investment projects, each worth around $20 million, and suggested the project with the best ROI

iv   Healthcare

- Increased patient satisfaction scores from 75% to 95% through a new service initiative
- Implemented a new system-wide performance management program, increasing productivity by 30%

- Reduced emergency room wait times by 25% through process improvements

v Sales

- Exceeded sales targets by 30% for three consecutive quarters
- Developed and implemented a new customer retention strategy, improving retention rates by 20%
- Negotiated a key account contract worth $2 million in annual revenue

vi Education

- Developed a new curriculum that improved standardized test scores by 15%
- Initiated a mentorship program that increased student retention rates by 25%
- Secured $500,000 in grant funding for innovative educational programs

Seamless Integration: Combining Achievements with Roles

When integrating achievements with job responsibilities:
- Start with a brief overview of your role and responsibilities
- Follow with bullet points highlighting your key achievements
- Ensure each achievement is relevant to the role and showcases transferable skills

Example:

Marketing Manager, XYZ Company (2018-2022)
Led a team of five in developing and executing marketing strategies for B2B clients.
- Increased client retention rate from 70% to 90% through targeted engagement campaigns

- Developed and implemented a social media strategy that grew followers by 200% in one year
- Spearheaded a rebranding initiative that resulted in a 25% increase in new client acquisitions

Crafting Powerful Achievement Statements

To create impactful achievement statements:
- Start with a strong action verb (e.g., "Implemented," "Developed," "Increased")
- Include a specific noun describing what you worked on
- Add a quantifiable metric to demonstrate impact
- Optionally, include the strategy or method used
- State the positive outcome or result

Example: "Implemented a customer feedback system (action verb + noun) using NPS methodology (strategy), increasing customer satisfaction scores by 35% (metric) and reducing churn by 20% (outcome)."

The Truth Matters: The Ethics of Achievement Reporting

Maintaining honesty in your resume is crucial. Fabricating achievements can have serious consequences:
- Risk of discovery during background checks or reference calls
- Potential termination if falsehoods are discovered after hiring
- Damage to professional reputation and future career prospects

Instead of bluffing, focus on presenting your genuine accomplishments in the most impactful way possible. If you're lacking in certain areas, consider how you can gain relevant experience or skills to bolster your resume honestly.

Tailoring Achievements to Job Descriptions

To make your achievements resonate with potential employers:
- Analyze the job description for key requirements and desired outcomes
- Match your achievements to these requirements
- Use similar language and terminology as the job posting
- Prioritize achievements that directly relate to the role's main responsibilities

Example: If a job emphasizes team leadership, highlight an achievement like "Led a cross-functional team of 10 members to deliver a critical project 15% under budget and ahead of schedule."

Remember, your achievements are a reflection of your professional journey. By thoughtfully presenting them, you create a powerful narrative that showcases your value to potential employers. Let your accomplishments speak for themselves, professionally and honestly, and you'll be well on your way to landing your dream job.

Key Points from Chapter 6: Showcasing Achievements – Crafting Your Professional Success Story

i The Importance of Achievements in Resumes

- **Differentiation:** Achievements set you apart from other candidates.
- **Value Proposition:** Highlight unique contributions to potential employers.
- **Credibility:** Provide concrete, quantifiable proof of success.
- **Storytelling:** Narrate your journey of problem-solving and innovation.

ii The Art of Humble Leadership

- Use **action verbs** like "Implemented," "Led," or "Developed."
- Focus on **results** rather than just responsibilities.
- Quantify achievements where possible (e.g., "Increased sales by 30%").
- Highlight team efforts using "we," while emphasizing your role.

iii Strategic Placement of Achievements

- **Professional Summary:** Feature standout accomplishments.
- **Work Experience:** Include 3-5 key achievements per role.
- **Skills Section:** Tie skills to measurable results.
- **Additional Sections:** Showcase freelance work or significant projects.

iv Using STAR and CAR Techniques

- **STAR:** Situation, Task, Action, Result.
- **CAR:** Context, Action, Result.
- Structure achievements to emphasize challenges, actions, and outcomes.

- Example: "Implemented inventory management system, reducing stockouts by 25% and boosting fulfillment speed by 15%."

v Making Achievements ATS-Friendly

- Use standard job titles and relevant keywords from the job description.
- Avoid complex formatting or graphics.
- Example: "Reduced costs by 20% through process improvements" aligns with ATS requirements.

vi Achievements for Freshers and Career Transitioners

- Leverage academic projects, internships, volunteer work, or personal projects.
- Example: "Developed a budgeting app, gaining 1,000+ users in three months."

vii Examples of Achievements Across Industries

- **Software Engineering:** Improved data processing speed by 40%, reduced security breaches by 97%.
- **Marketing:** Increased engagement by 75%, rebranding led to 25% growth in brand recognition.
- **Finance:** Managed portfolios outperforming indices by 10%, saved 15% in operational costs.
- **Healthcare:** Boosted patient satisfaction from 75% to 95%, reduced ER wait times by 25%.
- **Sales:** Exceeded sales targets by 30% for three quarters, secured a $2M key account.
- **Education:** Improved test scores by 15%, secured $500,000 in grants for innovative programs.

viii Integrating Achievements with Roles

- Briefly outline responsibilities, followed by bullet points showcasing key achievements.
- Example: **Marketing Manager**:
  - Led social media strategy, growing followers by 200% in one year.
  - Increased client retention rate from 70% to 90%.

ix Crafting Powerful Achievement Statements

- **Start** with an action verb.
- **Specify** what you worked on.
- **Quantify** results with metrics (e.g., percentages, revenue).
- **Highlight outcomes** (e.g., efficiency, cost savings).
- Example: "Developed CRM system, increasing customer retention by 25% and reducing churn by 15%."

x Maintaining Honesty in Reporting Achievements

- Fabrications can lead to termination, reputational damage, or failed background checks.
- Focus on genuine accomplishments and consider gaining relevant experience to bolster weaker areas.

xi Tailoring Achievements to Job Descriptions

- Analyze job postings for key priorities.
- Match achievements to job requirements using similar language.
- Highlight transferable and role-specific skills with measurable outcomes.

xii Conclusion

- Achievements are a powerful way to narrate your professional journey.

- Showcase them strategically, incorporating metrics and results.
- Tailor achievements to resonate with job descriptions and emphasize genuine, impactful contributions.
- Thoughtfully presented accomplishments can set you apart and significantly increase your chances of landing your desired role.

Chapter 6 – Quiz

1. **Why are achievements important in resumes?**
   a. They make resumes longer and more detailed.
   b. They provide measurable proof of your capabilities.
   c. They eliminate the need for a skills section.
   d. They are only necessary for leadership roles.

2. **What is the STAR technique for crafting achievements?**
   a. Skills, Tasks, Achievements, Results.
   b. Situation, Task, Action, Result.
   c. Strengths, Tactics, Actions, Results.
   d. Systematic Tracking and Reporting.

3. **How should achievements for freshers be highlighted?**
   a. Focus only on future goals.
   b. Emphasize academic projects, internships, or volunteer work.
   c. Avoid mentioning achievements if there's no work experience.
   d. Use achievements from unrelated hobbies.

4. **What is the best way to quantify achievements?**
   a. Avoid using numbers to keep the resume generic.
   b. Use vague statements that do not mention results.
   c. Include percentages, revenue, or time saved.
   d. Quantify only team achievements, not individual ones.

5. **What is a common mistake in reporting achievements?**
   a. Quantifying results with metrics.
   b. Using action verbs to start statements.
   c. Fabricating or exaggerating accomplishments.
   d. Aligning achievements with job descriptions.

Answer Key

1. b. They provide measurable proof of your capabilities.
2. b. Situation, Task, Action, Result.
3. b. Emphasize academic projects, internships, or volunteer work.
4. c. Include percentages, revenue, or time saved.
5. c. Fabricating or exaggerating accomplishments.

RESUME
EXPERIENCE
SKELLS
EXPERIENCE
SKILLS
EXPERIENCE
SKILLS
EDUCATION
SKELLS
SKILL'S
EDUCATION

DESIGNING VISUALLY APPEALING RESUMES

The ideal resume length varies depending on your career stage:

- Entry-level professionals: 1 page
- Mid-level professionals: 1-2 pages
- Senior executives or academics: Up to 3 pages

A standard resume structure includes:

- Contact information (header)
- Professional summary or objective statement
- Skills
- Work experience
- Education
- Additional sections (e.g., publications, awards)

Country-Specific Resume Preferences

United Kingdom (UK)

- Preference: Plain, professional layouts
- Term: "CV" is more common than "resume"
- Length: Typically 2 pages
- Photo: Avoid including photos due to anti-discrimination laws
- Popular layouts: Chronological, Functional, Combination

United States (US)

- Preference: Concise and achievement-oriented
- Length: 1 page for early-career, up to 2 pages for experienced candidates
- Photo: Discouraged due to Equal Employment Opportunity (EEO) laws
- Feature: Often includes a "Summary of Qualifications" section

Germany

- Preference: Detailed CVs with personal information
- Length: Can extend to 3 pages for senior roles
- Photo: Commonly included in the top corner

Middle East

- Preference: Comprehensive CV detailing all roles and achievements
- Length: 2-3 pages
- Photo: Frequently included

Crafting Key Resume Sections

Header
- Full name
- Professional title
- Email address
- City and country
- Phone number
- Relevant website links (optional)

Design tip: Use a clean font and ensure consistent alignment. Avoid decorative borders for ATS compatibility.

Personal Summary

- Length: 3-5 sentences or bullet points, not exceeding 150 words
- Content: Highlight top skills, experiences, and achievements relevant to the job
- Placement: Directly under the header

Skills Section

- Placement: Near the top, after the personal summary
- Content: List 5-10 key skills relevant to the job
- Format: Use bullet points or columns

Work Experience

For extensive work history:
- Limit each role description to 3-7 bullet points
- Focus on impressive, targeted achievements
- Keep each bullet point to two lines
- For multiple roles in one company, focus on key accomplishments

Education

- Placement: After professional experience for seasoned professionals; before experience for recent graduates
- Content: List degrees, institutions, and graduation dates
- Include certifications if applicable

Research Papers, Awards, and Publications

- Create a separate section titled "Publications" or "Achievements"
- Place near the end of the resume, before the education section
- Use bullet points to list titles and recognition
- Provide links to online publications where relevant

Design Considerations for Visual Appeal

Fonts and Spacing

- Font style: Use professional fonts like Arial, Calibri, or Times New Roman
- Font size: 10-12 points for body text; 14-16 points for headings
- Spacing: Use 1-1.15 line spacing for readability

Formatting Elements

- Use bold, italics, and underlining to break up text and improve readability
- Maintain consistent punctuation throughout the document
- Set margins to no less than 0.5 inches all around

ATS Compatibility Guidelines

To ensure your resume is ATS-friendly:
- Avoid using photos, borders, or graphics
- Use standard section headings (e.g., "Work Experience," "Education")
- Save your resume as a simple .docx or .pdf file
- Use a clean, simple layout without text boxes or columns
- Incorporate relevant keywords from the job description

Free AI-Powered Resume Templates

Several websites offer free AI-powered resume templates:
- Canva
- Zety
- NovoResume
- Resume.io
- Overleaf (ideal for academic CVs using LaTeX)

These platforms provide customizable, ATS-friendly templates with guided customization features.

Tailoring and Optimizing Content

- Customize your resume for each job application
- Use keywords from the job description throughout your resume
- Quantify achievements where possible (e.g., "Increased sales by 25%")
- Prioritize recent and relevant experiences
- Condense less relevant roles into a single "Additional Experience" section
- Use columns to save space while maintaining clarity

Final Checklist

Before submitting your resume, ensure:
- The resume is tailored to the specific job description
- Key achievements are quantified and concise
- The layout highlights critical sections for easy readability
- The design is ATS-compatible
- All information is accurate and up-to-date

Key Points from Chapter 7: Designing Visually Appealing Resumes

i Resume Length Recommendations

- **Entry-Level Professionals:** 1 page.
- **Mid-Level Professionals:** 1-2 pages.
- **Senior Executives or Academics:** Up to 3 pages.

ii Standard Resume Structure

- **Header:** Contact information.
- **Professional Summary:** Brief overview of qualifications.
- **Skills Section:** Highlight relevant capabilities.
- **Work Experience:** Showcase roles and achievements.
- **Education:** Include degrees and certifications.
- **Additional Sections:** Publications, awards, or projects as needed.

iii Country-Specific Preferences

- **United Kingdom (UK):** Plain layout, 2 pages, no photo, "CV" term used.
- **United States (US):** Concise, achievement-focused, 1-2 pages, no photo.
- **Germany:** Detailed CV, includes photo, up to 3 pages.
- **Middle East:** Comprehensive, includes photo, 2-3 pages.

iv Crafting Key Resume Sections

- **Header:** Include name, title, email, phone, city/country, and optional links.
- **Personal Summary:** 3-5 sentences summarizing skills and achievements.
- **Skills Section:** List 5-10 key skills in bullet points or columns.

- **Work Experience:** Use 3-7 bullet points per role; emphasize achievements.
- **Education:** Place appropriately based on career stage; include certifications.
- **Publications/Awards:** Use a separate section with bullet points.

v Design Considerations for Visual Appeal

- **Fonts and Spacing:** Use professional fonts (Arial, Calibri); 10-12 points for body text.
- **Formatting:** Bold, italics, and consistent punctuation improve readability.
- **Margins:** No less than 0.5 inches for ATS compatibility.

vi ATS Compatibility Guidelines

- Avoid photos, borders, graphics, or text boxes.
- Use standard section headings (e.g., "Work Experience," "Education").
- Save as .docx or .pdf files.
- Incorporate job-specific keywords.
- Opt for a clean, simple layout.

vii Free AI-Powered Resume Templates

- Platforms like **Canva, Zety, NovoResume, Resume.io**, and **Overleaf** offer customizable templates.
- Templates are ATS-friendly and designed for clarity.

viii Tailoring and Optimizing Content

- Customize resumes for each job application.
- Include keywords from job descriptions.
- Quantify achievements (e.g., "Increased sales by 25%").
- Highlight recent, relevant experiences.
- Use columns effectively to save space.

ix Final Checklist Before Submission

- Tailored to the job description.
- Quantified achievements are prominent.
- Layout emphasizes critical sections.
- ATS-compatible design.
- Information is accurate and current.

Conclusion

Designing a visually appealing resume requires balancing aesthetics with ATS compatibility. By tailoring content, quantifying achievements, and adhering to formatting best practices, you can create a resume that stands out to both digital systems and human reviewers. This thoughtful approach increases the likelihood of progressing to the next stage in the hiring process.

Module 7 – Quiz

1. **What is the recommended resume length for entry-level professionals?**
   a. 1 page.
   b. 2 pages.
   c. Up to 3 pages.
   d. As many pages as needed.

2. **Which country commonly includes photos in CVs?**
   a. United Kingdom.
   b. United States.
   c. Germany.
   d. None of the above.

3. **Where should the skills section typically be placed in a resume?**
   a. After the education section.
   b. Directly under the personal summary.
   c. At the end of the resume.
   d. Before the contact information.

4. **Which of the following ensures ATS compatibility in resumes?**
   a. Decorative borders and unique layouts.
   b. Graphics and text boxes.
   c. Standard section headings and clean formatting.
   d. Multiple font styles and sizes.

Answer Key

1. a. 1 page.
2. c. Germany.
3. b. Directly under the personal summary.
4. c. Standard section headings and clean formatting.

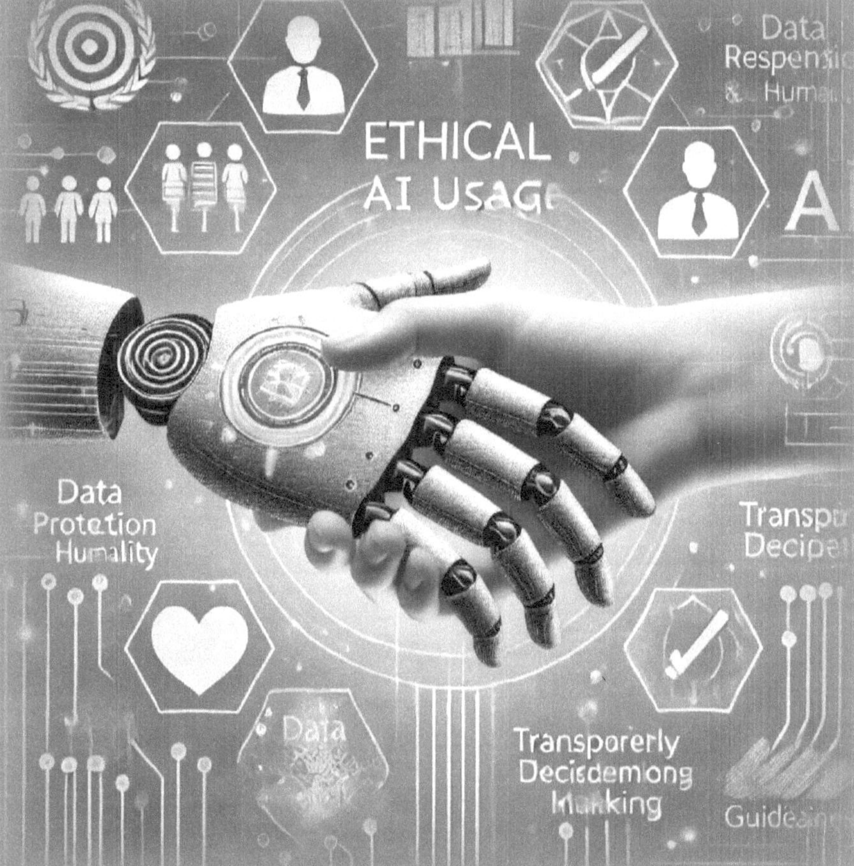

ETHICAL
AI USAGE
Data
Protection
Humanity
Transpa
Decipe
Data
Transparerly
Decisdemong
Marking
Guidea

ETHICAL AI USAGE

Transparency in AI-Assisted Resume Creation

Disclosing the use of AI in resume creation is becoming increasingly important in today's job market. Many hiring managers and HR professionals prefer candidates to be upfront about using AI tools in their application process.
This transparency builds trust and allows employers to better evaluate a candidate's genuine skills and experiences.

Striking the Right Balance with AI Dependency

While AI can be a powerful tool in resume creation, it's crucial to find the right balance between AI assistance and human input. Overreliance on AI can lead to generic, impersonal resumes that fail to capture a candidate's unique qualities.
A good rule of thumb is to use AI for initial drafting and optimization, but ensure that the final product reflects your personal voice and experiences.

The Irreplaceable Value of Human Touch

Human input remains critical in resume creation. AI may struggle with nuances, context, and the emotional aspects of a career journey.
Your personal experiences, achievements, and career aspirations are best articulated by you. The human touch adds authenticity

and helps create a connection with potential employers that AI alone cannot replicate.

Synergizing AI and Human Efforts

To effectively combine AI assistance with human input:
- Use AI for initial drafting and keyword optimization
- Review and edit the AI-generated content to inject your personal voice
- Add specific examples and achievements that showcase your unique experiences
- Ensure the final product aligns with your career goals and the job requirements

Streamlining the Resume Customization Process

For those needing to tailor multiple resumes daily, consider:
- Creating a master resume with all your experiences and skills
- Using AI tools to quickly adapt this master resume to specific job descriptions
- Developing templates for different industries or job types
- Allocating time for a final human review to ensure personalization and accuracy

Evaluating AI Resume Generators

Many websites claim to generate complete resumes at the click of a button. While these can be helpful starting points, they often produce generic results that may not effectively represent your unique qualifications

It's advisable to use these tools as aids rather than relying on them entirely.

Subscription Services vs. Open AI Platforms

Monthly subscriptions to specialized resume AI tools can be beneficial if you're in an active job search or frequently update your resume. However, similar results can often be achieved through smart usage of AI platforms like Claude, Perplexity, or ChatGPT-4. These general-purpose AI assistants can help with resume writing when given specific instructions and prompts.

Key Points from Chapter 8: Ethical AI Usage in Resume Creation

i Transparency in AI-Assisted Resume Creation

- Disclosing AI usage fosters trust and allows employers to evaluate a candidate's skills accurately.
- Transparency demonstrates integrity and ensures fairness in the hiring process.

ii Striking the Right Balance with AI Dependency

- **Role of AI:** Ideal for drafting, keyword optimization, and formatting.
- **Human Input:** Critical for injecting personal voice, context, and authenticity into the resume.

iii The Irreplaceable Value of Human Touch

- AI cannot fully grasp emotional nuances and context-specific career details.
- Personal experiences, aspirations, and achievements are best articulated by human effort.

iv Synergizing AI and Human Efforts

- Combine AI's efficiency with personal customization:
- Use AI for initial drafts and keyword optimization.
- Edit to align content with personal voice and experiences.
- Add specific examples and measurable achievements.
- Ensure alignment with job requirements and career goals.

v Streamlining Resume Customization

- Create a **master resume** encompassing all skills and experiences.
- Utilize AI tools to adapt the master resume for specific job descriptions quickly.

- Develop industry or role-specific templates to save time.
- Conduct a final human review for accuracy and personalization.

vi Evaluating AI Resume Generators

- **Advantages:** Useful as starting points for generating resumes.
- **Limitations:** Often produce generic results; require human refinement for individuality.
- Use AI tools as aids, not standalone solutions.

vii Subscription Services vs. Open AI Platforms

- **Subscription-Based Tools:** Offer specialized features for frequent job seekers.
- **General AI Platforms (e.g., ChatGPT, Claude):** Provide versatile, cost-effective assistance with well-crafted prompts.

Conclusion

Ethical AI usage in resume creation combines transparency, AI efficiency, and human authenticity. By synergizing AI tools with personal input, job seekers can produce compelling, tailored resumes that build trust and resonate with both ATS systems and human reviewers.

Module 8 – Quiz

1. **Why is transparency in AI-assisted resume creation important?**
   a. To reduce the cost of AI tools.
   b. To build trust with employers.
   c. To eliminate the need for human input.
   d. To increase reliance on AI tools.

2. **What is the best way to balance AI and human input?**
   a. Rely entirely on AI for resume creation.
   b. Use AI for drafting and humans for customization.
   c. Avoid using AI tools for resumes altogether.
   d. Use AI to automate the entire hiring process.

3. **What is a key limitation of AI in resume creation?**
   a. Inability to include keywords.
   b. Lack of understanding of emotional nuances.
   c. Difficulty formatting resumes for ATS.
   d. Failure to provide initial drafts.

4. **What is an effective strategy for tailoring resumes using AI?**
   a. Create multiple master resumes for different roles.
   b. Avoid using AI prompts for customization.
   c. Use AI to draft, then refine manually.
   d. Submit AI-generated resumes without edits.

5. **Which of the following is a benefit of general-purpose AI platforms?**
   a. They guarantee interview calls.
   b. They are versatile and cost-effective.
   c. They eliminate the need for customization.
   d. They replace the need for human judgment.

Answer Key

1. b. To build trust with employers.
2. b. Use AI for drafting and humans for customization.
3. b. Lack of understanding of emotional nuances.
4. c. Use AI to draft, then refine manually.
5. b. They are versatile and cost-effective.

AN EFFECTIVE
COVER
LETTER
COVER LETTER
E
COVER LETTER
COVER
LETTER

MASTERING THE ART OF WRITING AN EFFECTIVE COVER LETTER

A cover letter is often the first impression you make with a potential employer, and crafting one effectively can set you apart from other candidates. Here's a comprehensive guide to understanding, creating, and optimizing a cover letter that resonates with recruiters and hiring managers.

The Difference Between a Cover Letter and a Resume

While both documents are essential for a job application, they serve distinct purposes:

- **Resume**: A factual, structured summary of your skills, experiences, and education in a concise, bullet-point format.
- **Cover Letter**: A personalized narrative that contextualizes your qualifications, showcases your enthusiasm, and highlights why you are a perfect fit for the role.

Cover letters use a conversational tone, allowing you to explain career transitions, gaps, and achievements, while the resume remains formal and to the point.

Why Is a Cover Letter Important?

A cover letter plays a pivotal role in your application by:

- **Creating a Strong First Impression**: It's often the first document hiring managers read, providing an opportunity to stand out.

- **Demonstrating Enthusiasm**: It shows genuine interest in the role and organization.
- **Adding Depth to Your Application**: Offers context to your resume by elaborating on key experiences and achievements.
- **Showing Your Fit**: Highlights how your skills align with the specific job requirements and company values.

Employers use cover letters to assess soft skills, cultural fit, and your ability to communicate effectively.

Step-by-Step Guide to Crafting a Winning Cover Letter

i   Understand the Job Description

- Thoroughly read the job posting to identify key responsibilities, skills, and qualifications.
- Highlight keywords and phrases to include in your letter.

ii   Research the Company

- Familiarize yourself with the company's mission, values, culture, and recent achievements.
- Use this knowledge to personalize your letter and align your goals with theirs.

iii   Start with a Strong Opening

- Address the hiring manager by name whenever possible (e.g., "Dear [Name]").
- Craft an engaging opening sentence that grabs attention and expresses enthusiasm.

iv   Highlight Relevant Achievements

- Focus on accomplishments that align with the role.
- Use quantifiable results (e.g., "Led a team that improved productivity by 25%").

v   Align Your Skills with Job Requirements

- Match your qualifications with the job's needs using ATS-friendly keywords.
- Demonstrate how your background can solve specific problems for the organization.

vi End with a Call to Action

- Reiterate your interest and enthusiasm for the role.
- Politely request an interview or further discussion to elaborate on your qualifications.

vii Proofread and Tailor

- Review your letter for typos, grammatical errors, and flow.
- Ensure it's customized to the job and company.

How Long Should a Cover Letter Be?

A cover letter should be concise, typically **250–400 words**, and fit on a single page. It should include:
- A strong introduction.
- 2–3 focused paragraphs showcasing your achievements and skills.
- A compelling conclusion with a call to action.
Avoid overwhelming the reader with excessive detail.

Why You Should Customize Each Cover Letter

Generic cover letters often fail to make an impact. Tailoring your letter to each job application demonstrates:
- A genuine interest in the specific role and company.
- That you've taken the time to understand their needs and culture.

By aligning your skills and experiences with the job description, you show that you are an ideal candidate.

Using AI to Build a Cover Letter

Benefits of AI for Cover Letters

AI-powered tools can simplify the process by:
- Extracting relevant keywords and phrases from job descriptions.
- Generating structured drafts tailored to your resume.
- Providing suggestions for professional tone and phrasing.

How to Leverage AI Effectively

- Upload your resume and job description into an AI platform.
- Use prompts to generate an initial draft.
- Edit the draft to add personal touches and company-specific details.

AI Prompts for Creating an Effective Cover Letter

Here are some AI prompts to craft tailored cover letters:
- "Create a cover letter for [Job Title] at [Company Name] highlighting my key achievements from my resume."
- "Draft a cover letter showcasing my skills in [specific industry] while aligning with the job description."
- "Generate a professional cover letter that emphasizes why I'm the best fit for [specific role]."

Free AI Tools for Crafting Cover Letters

Here are some recommended tools for creating cover letters:

viii • **ChatGPT (OpenAI): Ideal for drafting personalized, professional cover letters.**

- **Zety**: Offers customizable templates and suggestions.
- **Novoresume:** Provides guided steps to create targeted cover letters.

- **Jobscan**: Focuses on ATS optimization with keyword suggestions.
- **Rezi**: Ensures ATS compliance and strong formatting.

Importance of ATS Keywords in Cover Letters

Incorporating ATS keywords improves the chances of your application being seen. To effectively use them:
- Analyze the job description to identify key terms.
- Naturally integrate these keywords into your letter.
- Avoid keyword stuffing, which can make your writing feel forced.

ATS optimization ensures your cover letter passes initial screenings, allowing your application to reach human reviewers.

Key Points from Chapter 9: Mastering the Art of Writing an Effective Cover Letter

i   **Understanding the Role of a Cover Letter**

- **Purpose:** A personalized narrative complementing the resume by providing context, showcasing enthusiasm, and highlighting fit for the role.
- **Differences from a Resume:**
- **Resume:** Structured and factual summary of skills, experience, and education.
- **Cover Letter:** Conversational and tailored, explaining career transitions, gaps, and achievements.

ii   **Importance of a Cover Letter**

- **Creates a Strong First Impression:** Often the first document recruiters read.
- **Demonstrates Enthusiasm:** Shows genuine interest in the role and organization.
- **Adds Depth:** Elaborates on key achievements and experiences.
- **Shows Fit:** Aligns your skills with job requirements and company values.

iii   **Steps to Crafting an Effective Cover Letter**

- **Understand the Job Description:** Identify key skills, responsibilities, and qualifications.
- **Research the Company:** Learn about its mission, values, and culture to personalize your content.
- **Start Strong:** Address the hiring manager by name and use an engaging opening sentence.
- **Highlight Relevant Achievements:** Focus on accomplishments that align with the role, using quantifiable results.

- **Align Skills with Job Requirements:** Incorporate ATS-friendly keywords and demonstrate problem-solving capabilities.
- **End with a Call to Action:** Reiterate interest, request an interview, and express enthusiasm for the role.
- **Proofread and Tailor:** Eliminate errors and ensure customization to the job and organization.

iv Ideal Cover Letter Length

- **Word Count:** 250–400 words, fitting on a single page.
- **Structure:**
- Strong introduction.
- 2–3 paragraphs showcasing achievements and skills.
- Compelling conclusion with a call to action.

v Customizing Each Cover Letter

- **Why It Matters:** Demonstrates genuine interest and alignment with the company's culture and needs.
- **How to Customize:** Align skills and experiences with job descriptions and use company-specific details.

vi Leveraging AI for Cover Letter Writing

- **Benefits:**
- Extracts relevant keywords from job descriptions.
- Generates structured drafts tailored to your resume.
- Offers professional tone and phrasing suggestions.

vii How to Use AI Effectively:

- Upload your resume and job description into the AI tool.
- Use prompts to generate an initial draft.
- Edit to add personal touches and align with the company's specifics.

viii Recommended AI Tools for Cover Letters

- **ChatGPT (OpenAI):** Drafts personalized, professional letters.
- **Zety:** Offers customizable templates with suggestions.
- **Novoresume:** Provides guided steps for tailored cover letters.
- **Jobscan:** Focuses on ATS keyword optimization.
- **Rezi:** Ensures ATS compliance with strong formatting.

ix Importance of ATS Keywords

- **Improves Visibility:** Ensures the cover letter passes ATS screenings.

x How to Use:

- Identify key terms in the job description.
- Integrate keywords naturally.
- Avoid overstuffing to maintain readability.

Conclusion

An effective cover letter complements your resume by providing a personalized narrative that highlights your fit for the role. By researching the company, tailoring content to the job description, and using AI tools for optimization, you can create impactful cover letters that resonate with hiring managers and improve your chances of landing an interview.

Module 9 – Quiz

1. **What is the primary purpose of a cover letter?**
   a. To replace the resume in an application.
   b. To provide a narrative showcasing enthusiasm and fit.
   c. To summarize educational qualifications.
   d. To include only ATS keywords.

2. **How does a cover letter differ from a resume?**
   a. It is less formal and includes career gaps.
   b. It avoids discussing achievements.
   c. It lists all work experience in bullet points.
   d. It excludes company-specific details.

3. **What is an ideal word count for a cover letter?**
   a. 100-200 words.
   b. 250-400 words.
   c. 500-600 words.
   d. Unlimited, depending on the role.

4. **What is a common mistake when crafting a cover letter?**
   a. Using specific achievements.
   b. Tailoring it to each job application.
   c. Being generic and not customizing for the role.
   d. Addressing the hiring manager by name.

5. **Which tool focuses on ATS keyword optimization for cover letters?**
   a. Canva.
   b. Jobscan.
   c. Zety.
   d. Novoresume.

Answer Key

1. b. To provide a narrative showcasing enthusiasm and fit.
2. a. It is less formal and includes career gaps.
3. b. 250-400 words.
4. c. Being generic and not customizing for the role.
5. b. Jobscan.

...

AI-dropanstunities
Opportunities in Job Search
Transforming Career opunities

AI DRIVEN OPPORTUNITIES IN JOB SEARCH: TRANSFORMING CAREER OPPORTUNITIES

The job search landscape has undergone a profound transformation with the advent of artificial intelligence (AI). This chapter delves deep into how AI is reshaping the process of finding jobs, refining applications, and enabling networking. From exploring advanced AI-powered job platforms to leveraging traditional and emerging tools, this comprehensive guide provides actionable insights for professionals navigating the competitive job market.

AI-Powered Job Search Platforms: Moving Beyond Traditional Portals

AI-powered job platforms are revolutionizing the traditional approach to job searching. Unlike popular job boards like LinkedIn, Indeed, Naukri, Bayt, and Monster, which predominantly focus on listing job openings, AI platforms use machine learning algorithms to offer personalized job recommendations, optimize applications, and streamline the search process. These platforms cater to specific career needs, saving time and providing better alignment between candidates and roles.

Examples of AI-Powered Platforms:

- **TalentAnywhere.ai**

This platform leverages AI to match candidates with jobs based on their skills, experience, and cultural fit. It provides basic job matching for free, while its paid tier ($19.99/month) includes features like resume optimization and AI-powered interview preparation. While TalentAnywhere excels in personalizing matches, it lacks the extensive job database of traditional platforms.

- **Eightfold.ai**

Focusing on deep learning, Eightfold.ai offers precise job matching and career path suggestions. Primarily catering to enterprises, it helps individuals align their skills with potential roles. Its enterprise-level pricing and focus on large-scale clients make it less accessible for individual job seekers.

- **Pymetrics**

This unique platform uses neuroscience-based games and AI to evaluate candidates' personalities and match them with suitable roles. It is free for job seekers, but its reach is limited to companies partnered with Pymetrics, narrowing its scope.

- **Hiretual**

Hiretual combines AI-powered talent sourcing with candidate engagement. Its free version provides basic searches and analytics, while advanced filters are available with paid plans starting at $99/month. It is particularly effective for finding niche roles, but the high cost of premium features is a drawback.

- **Wade & Wendy**

This AI-driven platform uses chatbots to provide personalized job recommendations and application assistance. However, its availability is restricted to companies in partnership with Wade & Wendy, limiting its utility for broader job searches.

These platforms provide an edge by tailoring job matches and optimizing applications, making them distinct from traditional job portals. However, their limitations include smaller databases, subscription costs, and occasional focus on enterprise users rather than individuals.

Leveraging Generative AI for Free Job Search Assistance

If subscription-based AI platforms are out of reach, tools like ChatGPT and Claude can be valuable alternatives. These language models can simulate AI-powered job search tools when used with carefully crafted prompts. By focusing on specific industries, job seekers can extract actionable insights, refine resumes, and even prepare for interviews.

Examples of Prompts for Various Industries:

- **Technology**: "Suggest current in-demand skills in cloud computing and cybersecurity, and how to highlight them in a resume."
- **Healthcare**: "Identify roles in healthcare management for candidates with 10 years of experience and relevant qualifications."
- **Finance**: "What certifications are essential for senior financial analyst roles, and how can I align my resume?"
- **Marketing**: "Find job openings requiring expertise in SEO and digital marketing for experienced professionals."
- **Legal**: "Provide insights into roles for intellectual property lawyers in the corporate sector."
- **Retail**: "List opportunities for retail operations managers with global experience."

- **Education**: "What skills are most valued for e-learning content developers?"
- **Environmental Science**: "Highlight growing career opportunities in sustainability and renewable energy."

Through tailored prompts, job seekers can use these tools to access industry-specific advice and insights, replicating many of the functions of premium AI job platforms.

The Role of Networking in the AI Era

While AI tools offer significant advantages, networking remains an indispensable part of the job search process. Building a strong professional network can lead to opportunities that may never be listed on job boards or AI platforms.

LinkedIn Premium: Enhancing Networking

LinkedIn Premium offers tools like InMail for direct communication, advanced search filters for identifying key professionals, and insights into who has viewed your profile. For $29.99/month, it enhances visibility and allows job seekers to connect with recruiters and decision-makers, making it an essential tool for professionals actively seeking roles.

DuckSoup: Automating Networking on LinkedIn

DuckSoup is a Chrome extension that automates LinkedIn profile visits, connection requests, and engagement. By analyzing your goals and suggesting personalized networking opportunities, it saves time and broadens your reach. Installation involves downloading the extension, linking it to your LinkedIn profile, and configuring automated settings. With plans ranging from free to $49.99/month, DuckSoup is a valuable addition to a proactive job search strategy.

Personal Branding: The Key to Standing Out

In a competitive job market, a strong personal brand is crucial. AI tools like **Grammarly** and **Canva** enhance communication and visual appeal, ensuring that resumes, cover letters, and portfolios reflect professionalism and creativity. Engaging with relevant LinkedIn groups, sharing thought leadership content, and participating in industry discussions can further strengthen your online presence.

AI Tools for Resume Building and Interview Preparation

Specialized platforms like **Jobscan** and **Rezi** ensure that resumes are ATS-compliant, improving their chances of passing automated screenings. For interview preparation, tools like AI-powered mock interview platforms provide practice sessions and actionable feedback, boosting confidence and performance.

Blending AI Tools with Traditional Strategies

The combination of AI-powered platforms, free tools, and traditional networking creates a robust job search strategy. While AI tools automate and personalize the process, human connections and branding provide the authenticity and adaptability needed to stand out.

Conclusion

AI has redefined the job search process, offering unprecedented personalization and efficiency. By integrating AI-powered platforms, leveraging generative AI tools, and enhancing networking efforts, job seekers can navigate the complexities of today's job market with greater ease and effectiveness. Balancing technology with traditional strategies ensures a holistic approach, paving the way for career success.

Key Points from Chapter 10: AI-Driven Opportunities in Job Search: Transforming Career Opportunities

i   The Shift to AI-Powered Job Platforms

- AI-driven platforms move beyond traditional job boards by offering:
- **Personalized Job Matches:** Tailored to skills, experience, and cultural fit.
- **Application Optimization:** Tools for resume refinement and interview preparation.
- **Efficiency:** Streamlined job searches through machine learning algorithms.
- **Examples:**
- **TalentAnywhere.ai:** Offers personalized matches and resume optimization.
- **Eightfold.ai:** Provides career path suggestions but focuses on enterprise users.
- **Pymetrics:** Uses neuroscience-based games for personality-role alignment.
- **Hiretual:** Excels in niche roles with advanced talent sourcing.
- **Wade & Wendy:** Chatbots assist with applications but are limited to partnered companies.

ii   Leveraging Generative AI for Free Assistance

- Tools like **ChatGPT** and **Claude** simulate premium AI platforms when used with targeted prompts.
- **Industry-Specific Prompts:**
- Technology: "Suggest in-demand cloud computing skills and resume tips."
- Healthcare: "Identify roles for healthcare management professionals."
- Marketing: "Find job openings requiring SEO and digital marketing expertise."

- **Applications:** Extract insights, refine resumes, and prepare for interviews.

iii Networking in the AI Era

- **Importance of Networking:** Provides access to hidden opportunities and enhances visibility.
- **LinkedIn Premium:**
- Features include InMail, advanced search filters, and profile insights.
- Cost: $29.99/month; enhances connections with recruiters and decision-makers.
- **DuckSoup:**
- Automates LinkedIn networking by managing profile visits, connection requests, and follow-ups.
- Cost: Free to $49.99/month, offering efficiency in expanding networks.

iv Personal Branding for a Competitive Edge

- **Why It Matters:** Reflects professionalism and makes candidates memorable.
- **AI Tools:**
- **Grammarly:** Enhances written communication.
- **Canva:** Creates visually appealing portfolios and resumes.
- **Strategies:** Engage in LinkedIn groups, share insights, and participate in industry discussions.

v AI Tools for Resume and Interview Prep

- **Resume Optimization:**
- **Jobscan, Rezi:** Ensure ATS compliance for higher visibility in screenings.
- **Interview Preparation:**
- AI-powered platforms offer mock sessions and actionable feedback to boost confidence.

vi Blending AI with Traditional Strategies

- **AI Contributions:** Automates job search, refines applications, and personalizes outreach.
- **Human Elements:** Networking and personal branding ensure authenticity and adaptability.

Conclusion

AI is transforming the job search landscape by enhancing efficiency, personalization, and reach. By combining AI-powered platforms, generative tools, and traditional strategies, job seekers can navigate the competitive market with confidence. Balancing technological innovation with human connections ensures a holistic approach to career success.

Module 10 – Quiz

1. **What is a key advantage of AI-powered job search platforms?**
   a. Larger job databases than traditional job boards.
   b. Personalization of job matches.
   c. Exclusive focus on entry-level roles.
   d. Free access to all advanced features.

2. **Which platform uses neuroscience-based games for job matching?**
   a. TalentAnywhere.ai
   b. Eightfold.ai
   c. Pymetrics
   d. Wade & Wendy

3. **What is the primary benefit of LinkedIn Premium in networking?**
   a. Offers free resume writing services.
   b. Enhances visibility and direct connections with recruiters.
   c. Automates application processes for all roles.
   d. Provides advanced ATS compatibility analysis.

4. **What AI tool can provide personalized prompts for job seekers?**
   a. Jobscan
   b. ChatGPT
   c. FairHire.ai
   d. HireVue

Answer Key

1. b. Personalization of job matches.
2. c. Pymetrics.
3. b. Enhances visibility and direct connections with recruiters.
4. b. ChatGPT.

CLEAR FOROATING
CLEAR FARMAING
TONCILSHOOTING
COMMON MESUAKES
SPELLING MISTAKES
QESDO
RESUME
CHECK FOR ERROLS
MISACANEGTED
CLEAR FORMATING
MISSING
ENSURE RELEVENCE
CLEAR FORMOATING
NESON DLTTONS
CHECK FOR ERRORS

TROUBLESHOOTING COMMON RESUME MISTAKES

This chapter equips you with tools and techniques to identify, fix, and prevent common resume mistakes. The content is divided into three main sections: identifying and fixing errors, optimizing grammar, formatting, and tone, and spot-checking AI-generated content for inaccuracies. Each section includes actionable steps, tools, and real-world examples to create polished resumes that stand out.

- **Identifying and Fixing Common Errors**

i   **Common Resume Mistakes**

- **Typos and Grammatical Mistakes**

- **Misspelled Words:**
- Example: Writing "manger" instead of "manager."
- Tip: Proofread carefully, as even small errors can hurt your credibility.

ii **Incorrect Grammar:**

- Lack of subject-verb agreement (e.g., "She write reports" instead of "She writes reports").
- Mixing tenses across roles (past tense for previous jobs, present tense for current roles).

iii Irrelevant Information

- Including hobbies that do not relate to the job.
- Listing outdated jobs or certifications beyond 15 years unless they're crucial.

iv Weak Descriptions

- Using vague terms like "helped improve processes" instead of "streamlined processes to reduce costs by 15%."
- Not including action verbs or quantifiable achievements.

v Inconsistent Formatting

- Uneven spacing between sections.
- Mismatched bullet styles or font types.
- Narrow margins or cluttered layouts that make reading difficult.

vi Overuse of Buzzwords

- Phrases like "team player," "dynamic," or "hardworking" are overused and lack impact unless supported by results.

How to Fix These Mistakes

Step-by-Step Process

i Use Spellcheck and Proofreading Tools:

- Tools: Grammarly, Hemingway App, Microsoft Word Spellcheck.
- **Pro Tip:** Read your resume aloud to catch awkward phrasing and typos.

ii Eliminate Irrelevant Content:

- Ask: "Does this information add value to my application?"

- Focus only on skills and experiences relevant to the job description.

iii Strengthen Descriptions:

- Replace generic phrases with action verbs and results:
  - Weak: "Improved sales."
  - Strong: "Increased sales by 20% within six months through targeted campaigns."

iv Fix Formatting Issues:

- Use a clean, professional resume template from tools like Canva, Zety, or Google Docs.
- Ensure consistent line spacing, bullet points, and margins (1–1.5 inches).

v Replace Buzzwords with Measurable Results:

- Instead of: "Strong team player," write: "Collaborated with a 10-member team to deliver projects on time, improving efficiency by 25%."

Optimizing Grammar, Formatting, and Tone

- **Grammar Optimization**

Common Issues
- **Passive Voice vs. Active Voice:**
- Passive: "Reports were prepared by me."
- Active: "Prepared reports for senior management."

- **Overusing Weak Verbs:**
- Replace "responsible for" with impactful verbs like "led," "designed," or "implemented."

Tools for Grammar Improvement

- **Grammarly**: Identifies grammatical errors and suggests fixes.
- **ProWritingAid**: Checks style, tone, and grammar clarity.
- **Microsoft Word**: Built-in grammar tools for basic checks.

- **Formatting Best Practices**

Key Elements

- **Professional Fonts:**
- Use easy-to-read fonts like Arial, Calibri, or Times New Roman.

- **Consistent Layout:**
- Keep font sizes uniform (e.g., 11–12pt for text, 14–16pt for headings).
- Avoid text boxes or tables, which can confuse Applicant Tracking Systems (ATS).

- **Effective Use of White Space:**
- Leave space between sections to improve readability.

Tools for Formatting

- **Canva**: Design templates for polished resumes.
- **Novoresume**: Provides ATS-friendly layouts and design tips.
- **Zety**: Offers easy-to-customize templates with clear section headers.

- **Adjusting Tone**

Professional and Tailored Tone

- Avoid casual language like "I crushed it at this role."
- Focus on achievements and skills using action-oriented language:

- Instead of: "I was in charge of the team," write: "Led a team of 12 to achieve a 30% growth in revenue."

Customizing the Tone

- Mirror the company's style:
- For corporate roles: Use formal, concise language.
- For creative industries: Be slightly more dynamic and expressive.

Spot-Checking AI-Generated Content for Inaccuracies

- **Common AI Errors**
- **Generic Statements:**
- AI-generated resumes often use vague phrases like "hardworking individual" without tailoring to the role.

- **Misrepresentation of Skills:**
- AI tools might list skills you don't possess (e.g., "Python expert" if you're only a beginner).

- **Logical Inconsistencies:**
- Overlapping dates between jobs or unrealistic achievements.

- **How to Spot and Fix AI Errors**

Steps to Identify Issues

- **Cross-Check with the Job Description:**
- Compare AI-generated content with the job posting.
- Highlight keywords that are relevant and remove irrelevant ones.

- **Verify Achievements:**
- Double-check metrics and achievements for accuracy (e.g., "reduced costs by $500K").

- **Simplify Over-Complicated Phrases:**
- AI tools may use overly complex language. Rephrase for clarity.

Refinement Tools

- **Originality.ai**: Detects AI-written content and flags inconsistencies.
- **ChatGPT or Jasper**: Use these tools to refine specific sections and improve clarity.

Practical Tools to Use

For Grammar and Spellchecking:
- Grammarly
- ProWritingAid
- Microsoft Word Spellcheck

For Formatting:
- Canva
- Zety
- Novoresume

For ATS Optimization:
- **Jobscan**: Matches your resume to job descriptions.
- **ResyMatch.io**: Analyzes ATS compatibility.

For Content Refinement:
- ChatGPT
- Jasper
- Hemingway App

Troubleshooting Checklist

Before submitting your resume, check the following:
- **Grammar and Spelling:**

- No typos or grammatical errors.

- **Achievements:**
- Quantified and relevant achievements included.

- **Formatting:**
- Consistent font, spacing, and bullet styles.

- **Tone:**
- Professional and tailored to the job.

- **AI-Generated Content:**
- Reviewed and personalized.

Key Points from Chapter 11: Troubleshooting Common Resume Mistakes

i   Identifying and Fixing Common Errors

- **Typical Mistakes:**
- **Typos and Grammatical Errors:** Misspelled words, incorrect grammar, or inconsistent tenses.
- **Irrelevant Information:** Hobbies or outdated jobs unrelated to the role.
- **Weak Descriptions:** Generic phrases lacking quantifiable achievements or action verbs.
- **Inconsistent Formatting:** Uneven spacing, mismatched fonts, and cluttered layouts.
- **Overuse of Buzzwords:** Phrases like "team player" without supporting results.

ii   How to Fix Mistakes:

- **Proofreading Tools:** Use **Grammarly** or **Hemingway App** and read aloud.
- **Content Relevance:** Remove unrelated details; focus on job-specific skills.
- **Enhanced Descriptions:** Replace generic phrases with measurable results (e.g., "Increased sales by 20% through targeted campaigns").
- **Formatting Consistency:** Use tools like **Canva** or **Zety** for clean layouts.
- **Replace Buzzwords:** Highlight actions and outcomes instead of overused terms.

iii   Optimizing Grammar, Formatting, and Tone

- **Grammar Improvements:**
- Use active voice (e.g., "Prepared reports" instead of "Reports were prepared by me").

- Avoid weak verbs like "responsible for"; use impactful ones like "led" or "implemented."
- Tools: **Grammarly**, **ProWritingAid**, or **Microsoft Word.**

iv **Formatting Best Practices:**

- Use professional fonts (Arial, Calibri).
- Ensure uniform font size (11–12pt for text, 14–16pt for headings).
- Leave ample white space for readability.
- Tools: **Novoresume**, **Zety**, or **Google Docs.**

v **Tone Adjustment:**

- Tailor tone to the company's style (formal for corporate roles, dynamic for creative fields).
- Focus on action-oriented language: "Led a team to achieve a 30% growth in revenue."

vi **Spot-Checking AI-Generated Content for Inaccuracies**

- **Common AI Issues:**
- **Generic Statements:** Vague phrases like "hardworking individual."
- **Misrepresented Skills:** AI may include skills you don't possess.
- **Logical Errors:** Overlapping dates or unrealistic achievements.

vii **How to Spot and Fix Errors:**

- Cross-check content with the job description and highlight relevant keywords.
- Verify metrics and achievements for accuracy.
- Simplify complex or unclear phrases for better clarity.
- Tools: **Originality.ai**, **ChatGPT**, or **Jasper** for refining content.

viii Practical Tools for Resume Troubleshooting

- **Grammar and Spellchecking: Grammarly, ProWritingAid, Hemingway App.**
- **Formatting: Canva, Zety, Novoresume.**
- **ATS Optimization: Jobscan, ResyMatch.io.**
- **Content Refinement: ChatGPT, Jasper.**

ix Troubleshooting Checklist

Before submission, ensure:

- **Grammar and Spelling:** Error-free content.
- **Achievements:** Relevant, quantified, and impactful.
- **Formatting:** Consistent font, spacing, and layout.
- **Tone:** Professional and tailored to the role.
- **AI Content:** Reviewed and personalized to reflect your voice.

Conclusion

Polishing your resume requires attention to grammar, relevance, formatting, and tone. By using AI and human effort in tandem, you can create an error-free, tailored resume that stands out to both ATS systems and recruiters. Regularly reviewing and refining your content ensures long-term success in job applications.

Module 11 – Quiz

1. **What is a common resume mistake related to formatting?**
   a. Using a functional format for all roles.
   b. Uneven spacing or mismatched bullet points.
   c. Highlighting quantifiable achievements.
   d. Including consistent margins.

2. **Which tool is most useful for optimizing grammar in resumes?**
   a. Canva
   b. Grammarly
   c. Jobscan
   d. LinkedIn Premium

3. **How can you strengthen weak descriptions in a resume?**
   a. Use more buzzwords like "team player."
   b. Avoid quantifiable results.
   c. Replace generic phrases with action verbs and metrics.
   d. Focus on unrelated hobbies.

4. **What is the purpose of spot-checking AI-generated resume content?**
   a. Ensuring ATS compatibility.
   b. Catching typos and grammatical errors.
   c. Verifying accuracy and personalizing content.
   d. Automating submission to job boards.

5. **What should you avoid when writing a resume?**
   a. Including action verbs.
   b. Tailoring content to job descriptions.
   c. Overusing generic buzzwords.
   d. Highlighting measurable achievements.

Answer Key

1. b. Uneven spacing or mismatched bullet points.
2. b. Grammarly.
3. c. Replace generic phrases with action verbs and metrics.
4. c. Verifying accuracy and personalizing content.
5. c. Overusing generic buzzwords.

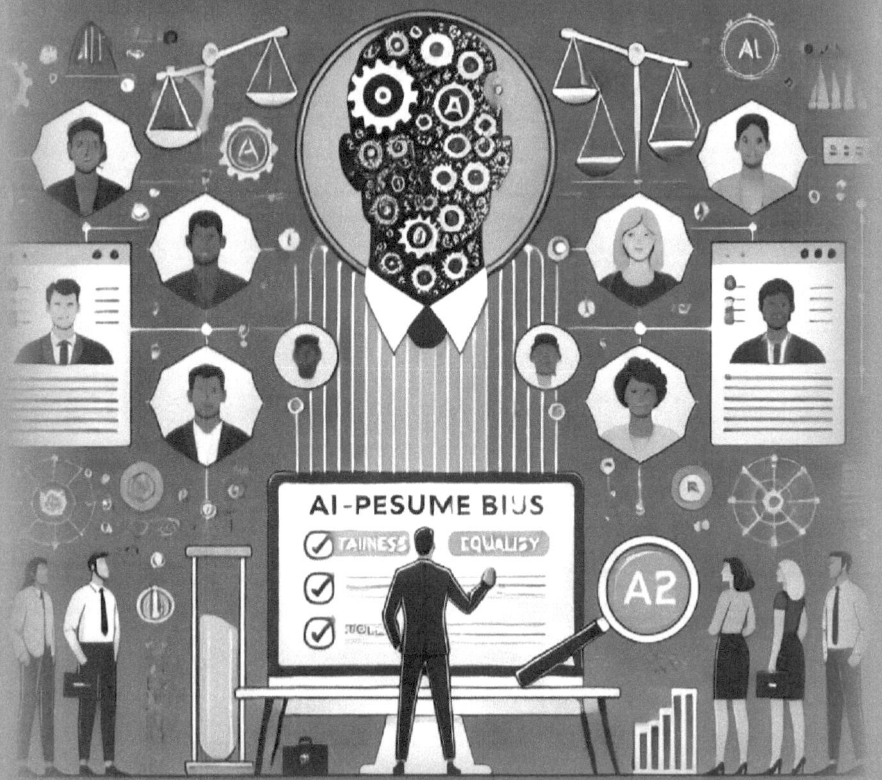
Oversoming AI Bias in Resume screenin
AI
AI-PESUME BIUS
TAIINESS
EQUALISY
A2

OVERCOMING AI BIAS IN RESUME SCREENING

- ## Introduction to AI in Resume Screening

AI in recruitment leverages algorithms to filter, rank, and shortlist candidates based on job descriptions and predefined criteria. While it enhances efficiency and reduces manual effort, it often replicates existing biases in hiring due to how it's trained. Addressing these challenges is crucial for both job seekers and recruiters to ensure fair and equitable opportunities. Job seekers need tools and strategies to make their resumes ATS-compliant while avoiding pitfalls caused by rigid AI filters.

- ## Understanding AI Bias

AI bias occurs when algorithms prioritize or exclude certain characteristics unfairly due to flawed training data or design. For instance, resumes with gaps or non-traditional formats are often deprioritized. Bias can stem from:
- Algorithmic Bias: Systemic preferences coded into the algorithm.
- Data Bias: Historical hiring patterns that favor certain demographics.
- Systemic Bias: Organizational practices influencing AI training.

Job seekers must recognize these biases and adapt their applications to navigate these barriers effectively.

- **Root Causes of Bias in Resume Screening AI**

AI bias originates from the data it is trained on and the algorithms designed to process that data. For example, if a company's past hiring favored men over women, AI trained on that data may replicate those patterns. Bias can also emerge from overemphasis on keywords, such as prioritizing "Ivy League" over equivalent qualifications. Employers must audit and diversify their data inputs, while job seekers can optimize resumes using tools like Jobscan to align with AI criteria.

- **Impact of AI Bias on Job Seekers**

AI bias disproportionately impacts candidates with career breaks, non-linear paths, or non-traditional education. For instance, a gap in employment for caregiving might lead to disqualification, even if the candidate is otherwise qualified. Similarly, candidates with diverse names or experiences may be filtered out. By using tools like TopResume to professionally tailor applications or LinkedIn Premium to network directly with hiring managers, job seekers can bypass some AI-imposed barriers.

Optimizing Resumes for AI Systems

AI screening tools often prioritize specific keywords and standardized formats. Use Jobscan:

- What It Does: Analyzes resumes against job descriptions for ATS compatibility.
- How to Use: Upload your resume and the job posting to receive a match score and keyword suggestions.
- Benefit: Highlights gaps and ensures alignment with AI expectations.

Leveraging Networking Tools

AI might filter out qualified candidates, so building relationships can help bypass these systems. Use LinkedIn Premium:
- What It Does: Connects you with recruiters and decision-makers directly.
- How to Use: Send personalized messages to hiring managers and showcase your expertise.
- Benefit: Reduces dependency on ATS, increasing chances of human review.

- ## How Employers Can Mitigate AI Bias

Employers play a critical role in ensuring fairness. Bias in AI tools can be minimized by:

Conducting Regular Audits
Tools like FairHire.ai assess hiring algorithms for bias:
- What It Does: Evaluates AI systems for fairness in decision-making.
- How to Use: Regularly review AI outputs and adjust parameters to correct imbalances.
- Benefit: Ensures inclusive hiring practices.

Combining AI with Human Oversight

Use platforms like HireVue:
- What It Does: Automates candidate pre-screening while providing human evaluators with unbiased insights.
- How to Use: Review AI-generated shortlists with human discretion for final decisions.
- Benefit: Balances efficiency with fairness.

Implementing AI-powered bias detection tools

Utilize specialized AI algorithms like Pymetrics:

- What It Does: Uses neuroscience-based games to evaluate candidates' soft skills.
- How to Use: Integrate it into your hiring process to assess candidates based on cognitive and emotional attributes.
- Benefit: Provides a more holistic view of candidates' abilities without relying on traditional metrics that may reinforce biases.

Leveraging AI for neutral job descriptions
Employ tools like Textio:

- What It Does: Scans job descriptions and suggests edits to remove gendered language.
- How to Use: Input your job descriptions into the platform for analysis and improvement.
- Benefit: Ensures job postings appeal to a diverse range of candidates, potentially increasing the diversity of your applicant pool.

Utilizing AI-driven semantic analysis

Implement tools like CVViZ that use natural language processing (NLP):

- What It Does: Parses resumes and extracts relevant information using NLP.
- How to Use: Upload resumes to the platform for comprehensive analysis.
- Benefit: Allows for a more nuanced evaluation of candidates' skills and experiences, going beyond simple keyword matching.

Implementing automated resume anonymization
Use AI tools like CloudApper AI Recruiter to anonymize resumes:

- What It Does: Automatically removes names, photos, and addresses from resumes.
- How to Use: Integrate it into your initial screening process to ensure unbiased first evaluations.
- Benefit: Ensures that initial candidate evaluations are based purely on qualifications and experience.

• Regulatory and Ethical Considerations

AI in hiring is governed by legal and ethical considerations to prevent discrimination. Employers should adhere to regulations like GDPR for data privacy and EEOC guidelines for anti-discrimination. Tools like Workday ensure compliance:
- What It Does: Provides end-to-end HR solutions while maintaining legal compliance.
- How to Use: Use integrated features for candidate data handling and bias checks.
- Benefit: Builds trust among applicants and ensures equitable practices.

• Role of Job Platforms and Third-Party Tools

For Job Seekers:

TopResume: Offers ATS-compliant resume writing services.
- How to Use: Submit your existing resume for professional rewriting tailored to job descriptions.
- Benefit: Maximizes AI compatibility and highlights key skills.

For Recruiters:

Greenhouse: Tracks candidate performance across the hiring funnel.
- How to Use: Analyze data to identify potential bottlenecks or biases in the screening process.

- Benefit: Improves hiring outcomes and promotes diversity.

- **Case Studies**

- Amazon's AI Failure: Their resume screening tool penalized the word "women's," highlighting the importance of auditing AI systems.
- Success Story: A mid-sized firm using Hiretual improved diversity hiring by leveraging AI to source candidates from underrepresented groups.

- **Future of AI in Resume Screening**

AI tools are evolving to reduce bias and better assess candidates holistically. Tools like Eightfold.ai focus on continuous improvement:
- What It Does: Uses deep learning to refine hiring practices and eliminate bias.
- How to Use: Integrate with existing ATS for bias-free candidate evaluations.
- Benefit: Promotes fair and inclusive hiring.

- **Actionable Tips for Job Seekers**

- Resume Tailoring: Use SkillSyncer to identify gaps in keywords.
- How to Use: Upload a job description and receive actionable recommendations for improvement.
- Benefit: Improves ATS ranking and keyword density.
- Professional Development: Showcase e-portfolios on platforms like Behance to highlight creative work.
- How to Use: Share links in applications to provide additional context.

• Conclusion

AI biases in resume screening can be mitigated by proactive job seekers and responsible employers. Applicants can use tools like Jobscan and LinkedIn Premium to optimize resumes and network effectively. Employers must invest in tools like FairHire. ai to audit systems and ensure fairness. By implementing AI-powered bias detection, leveraging AI for neutral job descriptions, utilizing semantic analysis, and automating resume anonymization, organizations can significantly reduce bias in their hiring processes. Together, these efforts can create a more inclusive and efficient hiring ecosystem.

Key Points from Chapter 12: Overcoming AI Bias in Resume Screening

i Introduction to AI in Resume Screening

- AI automates filtering, ranking, and shortlisting of candidates based on predefined criteria.
- AI systems can replicate biases from training data, impacting fair hiring.

ii Understanding AI Bias

- Algorithmic Bias: Preferences coded into algorithms.
- Data Bias: Historical hiring trends favoring certain demographics.
- Systemic Bias: Practices influencing AI design and training.

iii Root Causes of Bias

- Training data issues reflect past hiring biases.
- Over-prioritization of specific keywords excludes equally qualified candidates.

iv Impact on Job Seekers

- Candidates with career breaks, diverse names, or non-linear paths face exclusion.
- Use tools like **TopResume** for tailored, ATS-compliant resumes.

v Optimizing Resumes for AI Systems

- Use keywords from job descriptions.
- Standardize formats with tools like **SkillSyncer** and **Jobscan**.

vi How Employers Can Mitigate AI Bias

- Conduct regular audits with tools like **FairHire.ai**.
- Combine AI with human oversight using platforms like **HireVue**.

- Use AI-powered tools like **Textio** for neutral job descriptions and **CloudApper AI Recruiter** for anonymized resumes.

vii Regulatory and Ethical Considerations

- Adhere to GDPR and EEOC guidelines using tools like **Workday**.

viii Role of Job Platforms and Tools

- **For Job Seekers:** Use **TopResume** for ATS compatibility and **LinkedIn Premium** for networking.
- **For Recruiters:** Use **Greenhouse** to track and improve hiring processes.

ix Case Studies

- Amazon's AI penalized the term "women's," showing the need for audits.
- Firms like **Hiretual** improved diversity hiring with AI tools.

x Future of AI in Hiring

- Platforms like **Eightfold.ai** reduce bias and promote inclusive hiring.

xi Actionable Tips for Job Seekers

- Use **SkillSyncer** for ATS keyword optimization.
- Showcase skills and portfolios on platforms like **Behance**.

Conclusion

- Optimize resumes with tools like **Jobscan** and network proactively.
- Employers should audit AI systems and implement neutral hiring practices.
- A combined effort ensures equitable, efficient hiring.

Module 12 – Quiz

1. **What is a primary cause of AI bias in hiring?**
    a. Lack of human intervention in screening.
    b. Historical hiring data influencing AI training.
    c. Overuse of keywords by job seekers.
    d. Inclusion of diverse candidates.

2. **Which tool helps audit hiring algorithms for bias?**
    a. Jobscan
    b. FairHire.ai
    c. Resume.io
    d. HireVue

3. **How can job seekers optimize resumes for AI systems?**
    a. Avoid using keywords.
    b. Use outdated templates.
    c. Standardize formats and include relevant keywords.
    d. Focus only on networking.

4. **What role does LinkedIn Premium play in overcoming AI bias?**
    a. Automates resume customization.
    b. Increases access to decision-makers through direct
       networking.
    c. Provides bias-free job recommendations.
    d. Conducts audits on AI tools used by recruiters.

5. **Which of the following reduces bias in job descriptions?**
    a. CloudApper AI Recruiter
    b. Textio
    c. SkillSyncer
    d. Grammarly

Answer Key

1. b. Historical hiring data influencing AI training.
2. b. FairHire.ai.
3. c. Standardize formats and include relevant keywords.
4. b. Increases access to decision-makers through direct networking.
5. b. Textio.

AI TOOLS FOR PERFECT RESUMES: PLATFORMS, PROMPTS AND HACKS

- ## Introduction: The Role of AI in Resume Writing

AI has revolutionized the job search process by automating resume creation and optimizing content for Applicant Tracking Systems (ATS). Platforms like **Rezi, Zety, TopResume, Resume. io, Jobscan, TalentAnywhere.ai, ChatGPT**, and **Perplexity** offer tailored solutions to craft resumes that stand out. However, while these tools excel at automation, they lack the emotional intelligence and contextual understanding needed for crafting personalized, engaging resumes. This chapter explores how to effectively use these platforms, customize outputs with AI prompts, and streamline resume creation without compromising quality.

- ## Overview of Popular AI Tools

Rezi
- **What It Does**: Rezi is tailored for ATS optimization, offering real-time scoring, keyword suggestions, and industry-specific templates.
- **How to Use:**
- Upload your resume and job description.
- Use its ATS compliance checker to improve keyword usage.
- Export and finalize your resume.

- **Advantages**:
- Comprehensive ATS compliance feedback.
- Pre-filled templates for faster editing.
- **Pricing**: Free basic version; premium starts at $29/month.
- **Disadvantages**: Limited design flexibility.
- **Hack**: Save a master template and make quick edits for similar job descriptions.

Zety

- **What It Does**: Zety simplifies the resume creation process with a drag-and-drop editor and pre-written content suggestions.
- **How to Use**:
- Select a template and fill out sections using its AI suggestions.
- Export the resume and validate ATS compliance using Jobscan.
- **Advantages**:
- Intuitive user interface.
- Includes a cover letter builder.
- **Pricing**: Starts at $2.70 for a 14-day trial; $23.70/month thereafter.
- **Disadvantages**: Templates prioritize design over ATS compatibility.
- **Hack**: Pair Zety with Jobscan to ensure ATS optimization.

TopResume

- **What It Does**: Combines AI and human expertise to deliver tailored resumes.
- **How to Use**:
- Submit your resume for a free ATS review.
- Purchase a package for professional writing services.
- Collaborate with a writer to ensure personalization.
- **Advantages**:

- Professional human input.
- Industry-specific expertise.
- **Pricing**: Starts at $149.
- **Disadvantages**: Costly for frequent updates.
- **Hack**: Use the free ATS review to identify key improvements before making changes yourself.

Resume.io

- **What It Does**: A user-friendly platform for creating resumes with AI-driven suggestions and customizable templates.
- **How to Use**:
- Select a template and input basic details.
- Use AI suggestions to enhance your skills and experience sections.
- Export and review for relevance and ATS compatibility.
- **Advantages**:
- Multi-language support.
- Real-time improvement metrics.
- **Pricing**: $2.95 for a 7-day trial; $24.95/month thereafter.
- **Disadvantages**: Limited ATS-specific guidance.
- **Hack**: Best for creative industries or roles where design matters more than ATS compliance.

Jobscan

- **What It Does**: Focuses on ATS optimization, helping users match resumes to job descriptions.
- **How to Use**:
- Upload your resume and job description.
- Use its analysis to identify missing keywords and make edits.
- **Advantages**:
- Detailed keyword analysis.
- Provides an optimization score.
- **Pricing**: Free for limited scans; premium starts at $49.95/ month.

- **Disadvantages**: Limited free features.
- **Hack**: Use Jobscan for final validation after drafting your resume.

TalentAnywhere.ai

- **What It Does**: Focused on global recruitment, this platform emphasizes diversity hiring and custom recommendations for various roles.
- **How to Use**:
- Upload your resume for AI-driven analysis.
- Adapt recommendations to suit specific industries and cultural norms.
- **Advantages**:
- Diversity-focused insights.
- Tailored suggestions for global roles.
- **Pricing**: Custom pricing based on enterprise needs.
- **Disadvantages**: More recruiter-oriented than job-seeker-friendly.
- **Hack**: Use as a supplementary tool for international or niche roles.

ChatGPT

- **What It Does**: Generates resume content, including ATS-compliant skills, personal summaries, and achievements.
- **How to Use**:
- Provide clear, detailed prompts (examples below) to generate content.
- Edit outputs to match job requirements.
- **Advantages**: Fast and versatile.
- **Disadvantages**: Can produce generic content if prompts are unclear.
- **Hack**: Cross-validate ChatGPT outputs with Perplexity to ensure relevance.

Perplexity

- **What It Does**: Validates AI-generated content and provides insights into industry-specific trends.
- **How to Use:**
- Use prompts to cross-check skills, keywords, and trends.
- Refine content based on Perplexity's recommendations.
- **Advantages**: Keeps resumes aligned with current industry standards.
- **Disadvantages**: Requires effort to extract actionable insights.
- **Hack**: Pair with ChatGPT to enhance content quality and relevance.

- ## Using AI Prompts for Resume Creation

ATS Skills

- **Prompt**: "Extract 30 ATS-compliant skills for a [Role] from this job description."
- **Hack**: Combine ChatGPT outputs with Jobscan's keyword analysis for precision.

Personal Summary

- **Prompt**: "Write a 75-word summary for a [Role] emphasizing [Skills] and [Achievements]."
- **Hack**: Save summaries for similar job families, such as finance or healthcare.

Roles and Achievements

- **Prompt**: "Generate 5 quantifiable achievements for a [Role], focusing on measurable results."
- **Hack**: Test multiple prompts and save the most effective phrasing.

Industry-Specific Prompts

- **Technology**: "Write a summary for a software engineer specializing in AI and Python."
- **Healthcare**: "Draft achievements for a registered nurse, focusing on patient care metrics."
- **Finance**: "Generate skills for a financial analyst focusing on cost reduction and forecasting."
- **Marketing**: "Create a personal summary for a digital marketer, emphasizing campaign ROI."
- **Education**: "Draft roles for a high school teacher, focusing on student performance improvements."
- **Retail**: "Generate achievements for a retail manager, emphasizing sales and customer satisfaction."
- **Hospitality**: "Write a summary for a hotel manager, focusing on revenue growth and guest satisfaction."

Cross-Validation with Perplexity

- **Prompt**: "What are the top 5 skills for a [Role] in [Industry] in 2024?"
- **How to Use**:
- Paste ChatGPT outputs into Perplexity.
- Refine the resume using additional trends and skills identified by Perplexity.

Hacks to Save Time and Avoid Burnout

- **Save Prompts**: Create a library of tested prompts for recurring sections like skills and summaries.
- **Master Templates**: Develop templates for different industries and tweak specific sections for each application.
- **Batch Processing**: Customize multiple resumes in one session to save time.
- **Focus on Key Sections**: Edit only the personal summary, skills, and achievements for each job.

- **Work in Sprints**: Use 20-minute intervals to maintain focus and avoid fatigue.

- **Step-by-Step Process to Finalize a Resume**

- **Analyze the Job Description (5 minutes):**
- Use Jobscan to identify keywords and top skills.

- **Generate Content (10 minutes):**
- Use ChatGPT for drafting summaries, skills, and achievements.

- **Cross-Validate (5 minutes):**
- Verify accuracy and relevance with Perplexity.

- **Optimize for ATS (10 minutes):**
- Run the resume through Rezi or Jobscan.

- **Submit Applications (10 minutes):**
- Save and send tailored resumes.

Total Time: ~40 minutes per application.

Why Human Intervention is Critical

AI tools are efficient but lack the ability to:
- **Add Personality**: Resumes need storytelling to connect with recruiters.
- **Tailor Context**: AI cannot frame career gaps or unique achievements effectively.
- **Ensure Authenticity**: Over-reliance on AI can result in generic, impersonal resumes.

Example: AI might write, "Increased revenue by 20%," while a human can refine it to, "Implemented a targeted sales strategy that boosted revenue by 20% in six months."

Conclusion

AI tools like Rezi, Zety, TopResume, Resume.io, Jobscan, TalentAnywhere.ai, ChatGPT, and Perplexity have transformed how job seekers create resumes. These platforms offer powerful features, including ATS compliance, content generation, keyword optimization, and global recruitment insights. However, their true potential is unlocked when combined with human intervention. While AI excels at automating repetitive tasks and ensuring technical compatibility, only human expertise can add the contextual nuances, storytelling, and emotional resonance that resonate with recruiters.

By strategically using these tools and following the outlined hacks—such as saving tested prompts, leveraging master templates, and cross-validating with platforms like Perplexity—job seekers can create tailored resumes for each application in under 40 minutes. This approach not only maximizes efficiency but also ensures each resume stands out in a competitive job market.

The key takeaway? AI tools are invaluable assistants, but the final polish, personalization, and authenticity come from the human touch. By blending the strengths of both, job seekers can confidently navigate the modern hiring landscape and significantly improve their chances of landing their desired roles.

Key Points from Chapter 13: AI Tools for Perfect Resumes

i   Introduction

AI revolutionizes resume creation by automating ATS optimization and tailoring content through platforms like Rezi, Zety, TopResume, Resume.io, Jobscan, TalentAnywhere.ai, ChatGPT, and Perplexity. Human intervention remains essential for personalization and emotional resonance.

ii   Overview of Popular AI Tools

Rezi offers real-time ATS compliance feedback; save master templates for efficiency.

Zety provides pre-written content; pair with Jobscan for optimization.

TopResume combines AI and professional input; use free ATS reviews for refinement.

Resume.io excels in creative design; ideal for visually appealing resumes.

Jobscan focuses on keyword alignment; ensure ATS compatibility before submission.

TalentAnywhere.ai emphasizes diversity hiring; useful for niche and global roles.

ChatGPT generates content from prompts; validate outputs with Perplexity.

Perplexity aligns resumes with current industry standards.

iii   Using AI Prompts for Resume Creation

Prompts for ATS skills, personal summaries, and achievements enhance relevance. Examples include extracting skills for a role, drafting 75-word summaries, and generating quantifiable accomplishments.

iv   Cross-Validation with Perplexity

Use prompts like identifying the top five skills for specific roles to refine outputs.

v   Hacks to Save Time and Avoid Burnout

Save prompts, create master templates, batch-process resumes, focus on key sections, and work in short sprints to optimize productivity.

vi   Step-by-Step Process to Finalize a Resume

Analyze the job description with Jobscan, generate content using ChatGPT, validate relevance with Perplexity, optimize for ATS compliance using Rezi or Jobscan, and tailor resumes before submission.

vii Why Human Intervention is Critical

Human input adds personality, tailors context, and ensures authenticity, transforming generic AI-generated resumes into engaging and effective applications.

viii Conclusion

AI tools like Rezi, Zety, Jobscan, and ChatGPT enhance efficiency in resume creation. Combining these tools with human intervention ensures tailored, impactful resumes, providing job seekers with a competitive edge in modern hiring landscapes.

Module 13 – Quiz

1. **Which tool provides real-time ATS compliance feedback?**
    a. Resume.io
    b. Rezi
    c. Canva
    d. Zety

2. **What is a limitation of Zety templates?**
    a. Limited design flexibility.
    b. Overemphasis on ATS compatibility.
    c. Prioritization of design over ATS compliance.
    d. No support for creative industries.

3. **Which platform combines AI and human expertise for resume writing?**
    a. Jobscan
    b. Rezi
    c. TopResume
    d. TalentAnywhere.ai

4. **How can ChatGPT be effectively used in resume creation?**
    a. By automating all sections without human edits.
    b. By generating tailored summaries and ATS-friendly
       content.
    c. By creating graphics for resumes.
    d. By validating outputs through Jobscan.

5. **What hack can save time during resume creation?**
    a. Avoid customizing resumes for different jobs.
    b. Save tested prompts for recurring sections.
    c. Use only generic templates.
    d. Skip using AI tools.

Answer Key

1. b. Rezi.
2. c. Prioritization of design over ATS compliance.
3. c. TopResume.
4. b. By generating tailored summaries and ATS-friendly content.
5. b. Save tested prompts for recurring sections.

...

RESUME
ENTRY-LEVEL
RESUME
FRESH GRADUATS
Education
Skills
Internships
Internships
Achievemenes
RESUME

CRAFTING RESUMES FOR FRESH GRADUATES AND ENTRY-LEVEL ROLES

For fresh graduates and entry-level professionals, the challenge of building a strong resume lies in demonstrating potential and standing out with limited work experience. A well-crafted resume can make a lasting first impression in just 10 seconds and lead to interview calls. This module explores strategies, tools, and actionable steps to create a resume that effectively showcases your strengths.

- **Creating a Resume That Steals the Show in the First 10 Seconds**

Recruiters often skim through resumes quickly, so the first few seconds are critical. Here's how to capture their attention:

- **Use a Clear, Professional Format:**
- Select a clean template with clear headings and appropriate white space. A functional or hybrid format works well for entry-level resumes.
- Avoid overly designed resumes that distract from content.

- **Craft a Strong Career Objective or Summary:**
- This section should be tailored to the job description, highlighting key skills, education, and enthusiasm for the role.

- Example: *"Recent computer science graduate with expertise in Python and data analysis, seeking to contribute to innovative projects in a data analyst role."*

- **Place Key Skills Up Front:**
- Use the skills section to include both technical and soft skills relevant to the job. Match keywords from the job description.

- **Quantify Achievements Early:**
- Showcase internships, academic projects, or volunteer work using metrics to illustrate impact.
- Example: *"Developed a marketing strategy during an internship that increased social media engagement by 30%."*

- **Tailor Each Resume:**
- Personalize your resume for every job application by incorporating relevant keywords and emphasizing applicable experiences.

- **Building Resumes with Limited Work Experience**

When you don't have a robust work history, focus on what you *do* have:

- **Education:**

Highlight your degree, major, relevant coursework, and any academic honors or awards. If your GPA is impressive, include it.

- **Skills:**

Showcase hard skills (e.g., data analysis, coding, languages) and soft skills (e.g., communication, problem-solving).

- **Academic Projects:**

Treat significant academic work like mini job experiences. Describe your role, the tools/technologies you used, and measurable outcomes.

- **Internships and Volunteer Work:**

These experiences can demonstrate your ability to apply knowledge practically. Use action verbs to describe your contributions.

- **Highlighting Academic Projects, Internships, and Volunteer Work**

Even without a job history, you can showcase your value through impactful descriptions:

- **Academic Projects:**

Describe projects using measurable outcomes and skills used. Example: *"Led a team of 5 to develop a web app that improved task efficiency by 20%."*

- **Internships:**

Focus on contributions and the skills you gained. Example: *"Streamlined onboarding processes during an internship, reducing completion time by 25%."*

- **Volunteer Work:**

Highlight transferable skills like leadership and communication. Example: *"Managed logistics for a charity event that raised $10,000."*

- **Using AI Tools to Stand Out**

AI tools can enhance your resume by making it polished, ATS-compliant, and tailored:

- **AI Tools to Use:**
- **Jobscan:** Identifies ATS keywords for optimization.
- **Grammarly:** Ensures professional tone and grammar.
- **Canva:** Offers visually appealing resume templates.
- **ChatGPT:** Helps generate tailored summaries, skills, and content.

- **AI Prompts:**
- *"Create a career objective for a recent business graduate seeking a role in marketing."*
- *"Generate 5 measurable bullet points for an internship in social media management."*
- *"List 10 ATS-compliant skills for an entry-level data analyst role."*

- **How to Stand Out Without Work Experience**

- **Emphasize Initiative:**

Include certifications, online courses, or self-taught skills to demonstrate your drive.

- **Use a Portfolio:**

If applicable, link to a portfolio, GitHub, or LinkedIn profile showcasing your work.

- **Highlight Transferable Skills:**

Time management, teamwork, and problem-solving are valuable in any industry.

- **Quantify Achievements:**

Use numbers to demonstrate impact, even in academic or volunteer roles.

- **How to Cover Career Gaps Without Lying**

- **Focus on Skill Development:**

Highlight certifications, freelancing, or personal projects completed during the gap.

- **Use a Functional Format:**

This focuses on skills rather than chronological experience.

- **Address Gaps Briefly:**

In a cover letter or interview, frame gaps as periods of growth or skill-building.
Example: *"Spent time pursuing certifications in web development to enhance my technical expertise."*

- **What to Include in Your Resume**

- **Contact Information:**

Ensure your email and LinkedIn profile are professional.

- **Objective or Summary:**

A tailored, concise statement demonstrating enthusiasm and alignment with the role.

- **Skills Section:**

List relevant skills using keywords from the job description.

- **Experience:**

Highlight internships, volunteer work, or projects. Use action verbs and metrics.

- **Education:**

Include coursework and achievements relevant to the role.

- **Certifications and Awards:**

Showcase your commitment to continuous learning.

- **What Not to Include**

- **Irrelevant Personal Information:**

Avoid marital status, age, or a photo in regions where it's unnecessary.

- **Typos or Errors:**

Proofread to maintain a professional impression.

- **Unrelated Experiences:**

Focus on roles or activities that highlight transferable skills.

- **Generic Objectives:**

Tailor your objective to each job application.

- **Strategies to Increase Interview Calls**

- **Optimize for ATS:**

Use job-specific keywords in your skills and experience sections.

- **Customize Every Resume:**

Tailor each resume to the specific job description.

- **Leverage Networking:**

Connect with professionals in your target industry via LinkedIn.

- **Follow-Up:**

After applying, follow up with a polite email expressing interest in the role.

- **Stay Consistent:**

Apply to multiple roles regularly, refining your resume based on feedback.

By using these strategies and tools, fresh graduates and entry-level candidates can create resumes that effectively showcase their potential and increase their chances of landing interviews. Remember, the goal is to demonstrate what you *can do* by leveraging your skills, education, and enthusiasm.

Key Points from Chapter 14: Crafting Resumes for Fresh Graduates and Entry-Level Roles

i First Impressions Matter:

- A resume should captivate attention in 10 seconds with a professional format, tailored objectives, and quantifiable achievements.

ii Focus on Potential:

- Highlight education, skills, academic projects, internships, and volunteer work to compensate for limited work experience.

iii Tailored Resumes:

- Customize each resume to the job description using relevant keywords and emphasizing applicable skills.

iv Leverage AI Tools:

- Use platforms like Jobscan for ATS optimization, Grammarly for professional tone, and Canva for visual appeal.

v Quantify Achievements:

- Demonstrate impact through metrics even in academic or volunteer roles (e.g., "Increased engagement by 30%").

vi Cover Career Gaps Positively:

- Frame gaps as periods of skill development and growth, and use functional formats to emphasize abilities.

vii Avoid Common Mistakes:

- Eliminate typos, irrelevant details, and generic objectives for a polished, job-specific resume.

viii Strategies to Secure Interviews:

- Optimize for ATS, leverage LinkedIn for networking, and consistently apply to roles with tailored resumes.

By emphasizing education, skills, and achievements, and leveraging modern tools, fresh graduates can create compelling resumes that open doors to professional opportunities.

Module 14 – Quiz

1. **What should a career objective for fresh graduates include?**
   a. Generic goals.
   b. Tailored skills, education, and enthusiasm.
   c. A detailed professional history.
   d. Unrelated hobbies.

2. **What is the best way to present academic projects on a resume?**
   a. Use measurable outcomes and relevant skills.
   b. Include vague details without specifics.
   c. Highlight projects only from the first year of study.
   d. Avoid mentioning group contributions.

3. **Which tool can help fresh graduates optimize resumes for ATS?**
   a. Canva
   b. Grammarly
   c. Jobscan
   d. ChatGPT

4. **What is an effective strategy for covering career gaps?**
   a. Exaggerate work experience.
   b. Highlight skill-building activities during the gap.
   c. Leave the gap unexplained.
   d. Avoid applying for jobs that require explanations.

5. **What is one thing fresh graduates should avoid including on resumes?**
   a. Quantifiable achievements.
   b. Irrelevant personal information.
   c. Tailored career objectives.
   d. Transferable skills.

Answer Key

1. b. Tailored skills, education, and enthusiasm.
2. a. Use measurable outcomes and relevant skills.
3. c. Jobscan.
4. b. Highlight skill-building activities during the gap.
5. b. Irrelevant personal information.

CRAFTING RESUME
FOR SENIOR LEADERSHIP ROLES
LEADERSHIP EXPERIENCE
FOR SENIOR LEADERSHIP ROLES
LEADERSHIP EXPERIENCE
LEADERSHIP EXPERIENCE
STRATEGIC VISION
ACHIETEGIC VISION
SKILLS
LEADEESHIP EXPERIENCE

RESUMES FOR SENIOR LEADERSHIP ROLES

Creating a resume for executive roles such as CEO, VP, or Director requires a strategic, results-driven approach. This module combines insights from leading sources to provide a comprehensive guide on crafting an impactful resume for senior leadership positions. It covers key elements such as standing out, ideal length, structuring content, and using AI tools to refine your resume.

How to Stand Out and Be Unique

Senior leadership resumes need to leave a lasting impression within seconds. Here's how:

- **Position Yourself as a Strategic Leader:**

Demonstrate how you've driven measurable organizational growth through strategic initiatives. Highlight visionary achievements that set you apart.
Example: *"Spearheaded a $20M digital transformation initiative, increasing operational efficiency by 30%."*

- **Showcase Thought Leadership:**

Include evidence of your influence through publications, keynote speeches, and industry panels. Mention leadership on boards or advisory groups.
Example: *"Keynote speaker at the Global Tech Summit, sharing insights on AI-driven innovation."*

- **Focus on Metrics and Outcomes:**

Quantify your accomplishments to provide a clear picture of your impact.
Example: *"Increased market share by 15% over three years through a customer-centric marketing strategy."*

- **Craft a Bold Executive Summary:**

Your summary should succinctly capture your career achievements, leadership style, and unique contributions.
Example: *"Transformational executive with 25+ years of experience driving innovation, profitability, and operational excellence across global markets."*

- **Ideal Resume Length for Senior Leaders**

Executive resumes need to be comprehensive yet concise, typically spanning **two pages**:

- **Focus on the Last 10–15 Years:**

Highlight recent and relevant roles that demonstrate leadership. Older experiences can be summarized briefly.

- **Use a Career Highlights Section:**

Summarize key accomplishments from earlier roles in a concise, impactful format.
Example: *"Early Career Highlights: Streamlined global logistics operations, reducing costs by $10M annually."*

- **When a Three-Page Resume is Acceptable:**

A third page may be justified for candidates with extensive global experience or multiple board appointments, but ensure the content remains relevant and impactful.

- ## **Including or Skipping Years of Hard Work**

Your resume should reflect your career trajectory without overwhelming the reader:

- ### **Summarize Early Career Roles:**

Group earlier positions under a general heading such as *"Additional Leadership Experience"* with key highlights in bullet points.

- ### **Emphasize Career Growth:**

Highlight promotions or role transitions to illustrate progression. Example: *"Promoted to VP of Operations after consistently exceeding revenue targets by 25% annually."*

- ### **Focus on Results, Not Tenure:**

Replace time-based descriptions with achievement-focused narratives.
Example: *"Led a turnaround strategy that achieved profitability within 18 months, increasing revenue by 40%."*

- ### **Building a Consolidated Resume for Multiple Roles**

Senior leaders often apply to diverse roles and need a versatile yet impactful resume:

- ### **Create a Master Resume:**

Start with a detailed document that includes all roles, achievements, metrics, and projects. Use this as a foundation to tailor applications quickly.

- ### **Prioritize Key Themes:**

Focus on universally valued leadership traits like innovation, stakeholder management, and strategic vision.

- **Use Keywords Intelligently:**

Incorporate keywords like *"enterprise growth," "stakeholder engagement," and "global transformation"* to appeal to ATS systems while maintaining relevance.

- ## **Structure for a Full-Proof Resume**

A senior leadership resume must be clear, compelling, and professionally structured:

- **Header:**

Include your name, title (e.g., *"Chief Executive Officer"*), contact information, and LinkedIn or portfolio links.

- **Executive Summary:**

Summarize your career highlights in 3–4 impactful lines, focusing on strategic outcomes.

- **Core Competencies:**

Include a skills section tailored to the role, e.g., *"Change Management, Strategic Planning, Market Expansion."*

- **Professional Experience:**
- Use reverse chronological order.
- Highlight key achievements with action verbs and measurable outcomes.
- Example: *"Directed a $100M acquisition, achieving seamless integration and 20% ROI in 18 months."*

- **Education:**

Include advanced degrees, certifications, and executive programs.

- **Board Memberships and Affiliations:**

List leadership roles on advisory boards or professional organizations.

- **Publications and Thought Leadership:**

Highlight relevant articles, books, and speaking engagements to demonstrate influence.

- **Words and Phrases to Use**

Use strong, action-oriented language to convey authority and strategic insight:

- **Leadership Verbs:**

Spearheaded, Championed, Directed, Accelerated, Pioneered, Negotiated.

- **Strategic Metrics:**

Increased EBITDA, Reduced churn, Enhanced stakeholder value, Optimized costs.

- **Visionary Phrases:**

"Catalyzed industry disruption by leveraging advanced analytics." *"Fostered organizational agility through transformative leadership initiatives."*

- **What Makes a Resume Magnetic**

A magnetic resume immediately grabs attention with these elements:

- **Results Over Responsibilities:**

Focus on outcomes rather than tasks.

Example: Replace *"Oversaw marketing strategy"* with *"Developed a marketing strategy that increased lead conversion by 35%."*

- **Incorporate Testimonials:**

Use a quote or endorsement from a performance review or board member.

Example: *"'A visionary leader with an unparalleled ability to drive change' – Board Member, ABC Corp."*

- **Visually Appealing Design:**

Use bold headings, bullet points, and ample white space to improve readability.

- ## AI Tools for Senior Leaders

AI tools can help refine senior leadership resumes, but they should complement your unique voice:
- **Zety**: Offers professional templates tailored for executive roles.
- **TealHQ**: Customizes resumes based on job descriptions.
- **Jobscan**: Ensures ATS compliance by analyzing keywords.
- **LinkedIn AI Profile Optimizer**: Aligns your LinkedIn profile with your resume.
- **Grammarly Premium**: Polishes grammar and style for executive-level communication.

- ## Tips for Creating a Foolproof Resume

- **Invest in a Professional Resume Writer:**

A professional can tailor your resume to emphasize leadership qualities and strategic vision.

- **Focus on Evergreen Skills:**

Highlight traits like adaptability, stakeholder management, and global leadership.

- **Keep It Updated:**

Regularly refresh your resume with recent accomplishments and roles.

- **Proofread Meticulously:**

Typos and inconsistencies are unacceptable at this level. Use professional editing tools or a trusted peer for review.

By following these guidelines, senior leaders can craft a consolidated, high-impact resume that showcases their leadership capabilities, strategic vision, and thought leadership.

Key Points from Chapter 15: Resumes for Senior Leadership Roles

i   Strategic Positioning:

- Senior leadership resumes should emphasize strategic achievements, thought leadership, and measurable outcomes. Examples include driving revenue growth, spearheading transformation initiatives, or increasing market share.

ii   Bold Executive Summary:

- Craft a succinct summary showcasing leadership style, achievements, and unique contributions. Focus on key outcomes to leave a strong first impression.

iii   Metrics-Driven Impact:

- Use quantifiable accomplishments to highlight influence, such as boosting EBITDA, enhancing operational efficiency, or reducing costs through strategic initiatives.

iv   Tailored Resume Length:

- Typically two pages, with a third allowed for extensive global experience. Highlight recent roles and consolidate earlier experiences into a career highlights section.

v   Clear Structure:

- Use professional formatting, including sections for executive summaries, core competencies, professional experience, education, board memberships, and publications.

vi   Leadership Language:

- Incorporate action-oriented and visionary phrases like "spearheaded," "optimized," or "catalyzed industry disruption" to convey authority and insight.

vii Magnetic Elements:

- Focus on results over responsibilities, incorporate testimonials, and maintain visually appealing, readable formatting.

viii AI Tools for Refinement:

- Leverage platforms like Jobscan for ATS compliance, Grammarly for style and grammar, and LinkedIn optimizers for consistent branding.

ix Invest in Professional Assistance:

- Work with resume writers and trusted peers for proofreading, ensuring the document reflects senior-level expertise.

Module 15 – Quiz

1. **What should a senior leadership resume emphasize to stand out?**
   a. Generic skills and experiences.
   b. Strategic achievements and measurable outcomes.
   c. Day-to-day responsibilities.
   d. Personal hobbies.

2. **What is the ideal length for a senior leadership resume?**
   a. One page.
   b. Two pages, with a third for extensive experience.
   c. Three pages, always.
   d. Unlimited.

3. **What should be included in the Career Highlights section?**
   a. Detailed descriptions of all past roles.
   b. Personal interests and hobbies.
   c. Summarized key accomplishments from earlier roles.
   d. A comprehensive timeline of career history.

4. **What makes an effective Executive Summary for senior leaders?**
   a. Listing all past employers.
   b. Highlighting strategic vision, leadership style, and key outcomes.
   c. Describing technical skills in detail.
   d. Sharing personal anecdotes.

5. **Which of these reflects thought leadership on a senior leadership resume?**
    a. Participated in weekly team meetings.
    b. Managed daily team operations effectively.
    c. Delivered a keynote speech at an industry conference.
    d. Assisted in organizing a company event.

6. **Which action-oriented word is best suited for a senior leadership resume?**
    a. Oversaw.
    b. Spearheaded.
    c. Attempted.
    d. Observed.

Answer Key for Chapter 15

1. b. Strategic achievements and measurable outcomes.
2. b. Two pages, with a third for extensive experience.
3. c. Summarized key accomplishments from earlier roles.
4. b. Highlighting strategic vision, leadership style, and key outcomes.
5. c. Delivered a keynote speech at an industry conference.
6. b. Spearheaded.

Future trends in
AI Resume Building
DATA ANALYTICS
MACHINE LEARNING
RESUME Algorithms
Datine Analytics
DATA ANALYTICS
Data Analytics
Cagonile Iersonizing Iersonine Resumes
learning Resumes
RESUME
AI
RESUME
DATE

FUTURE TRENDS IN AI AND RESUME BUILDING

The integration of Artificial Intelligence (AI) in resume building and job applications is revolutionizing the hiring process. This chapter explores the emerging trends, technologies, and strategies that job seekers can leverage to stay competitive in an AI-driven landscape. By understanding these developments, candidates can craft compelling resumes, navigate evolving hiring practices, and position themselves as forward-thinking professionals.

- ## AI-Generated Content Enhancement

AI tools are becoming indispensable for enhancing resume content. These systems analyze job descriptions, highlight essential keywords, and tailor resumes to specific roles.

- **Custom Tailoring with AI:**

AI platforms like Rezi and Jobscan optimize resumes for Applicant Tracking Systems (ATS) by aligning keywords with job descriptions.
Example: For a digital marketing role, the tool might emphasize skills like "SEO optimization" and "content strategy."

- **Automated Section Generation:**

Generative AI tools can create impactful summaries, experience descriptions, and skills sections, saving time for job seekers.

Example: ChatGPT can draft a professional summary highlighting leadership and technical expertise.

- ## Dynamic Portfolio Integration

Static resumes are being replaced by dynamic, AI-enabled portfolios that ensure applications remain up-to-date and compelling.

- **Real-Time Updates:**

AI tools can sync with personal achievements, automatically adding new certifications, projects, and skills to digital resumes. Example: An AI-powered portfolio updates itself with certifications like Google Analytics or Salesforce upon completion.

- **Interactive Formats:**

Digital portfolios link to work samples, video introductions, and case studies, giving employers a holistic view of the candidate's abilities.

- ## Predictive Analytics for Skill Gaps

AI-powered tools are increasingly providing predictive insights to help job seekers identify and fill skill gaps:

- **Skill Recommendations:**

Based on industry trends, AI tools suggest skills to acquire for future roles.
Example: A data scientist might be advised to learn emerging technologies like AI ethics or quantum computing.

- **Proactive Learning:**

Platforms like LinkedIn Learning integrate with predictive analytics, recommending courses aligned with career goals.

- ## ATS Optimization Algorithms

AI tools are addressing the critical challenge of passing ATS filters, which screen over 60% of resumes before they reach human recruiters:

- ### Keyword Analysis:

AI analyzes job descriptions to identify and recommend relevant keywords for inclusion.
Example: For a project management role, terms like "Agile methodology" and "budget management" are flagged as essential.

- ### Template Optimization:

Tools like Teal and VisualCV ensure that resumes are formatted to meet ATS requirements without compromising readability.

- ## Visual Resume Builders

AI-powered visual resume builders are enhancing design while maintaining professional readability:
- ### Automated Layout Selection:
AI tools suggest colors, fonts, and layouts tailored to industries, making resumes visually appealing yet formal.
Example: A creative role might feature bold colors and modern layouts, while a corporate role opts for minimalist design.

- ### Infographics and Charts:

Interactive elements like skill charts and career timelines help candidates visually showcase their expertise.

- ## AI-Powered Video Resumes

Video resumes are emerging as an impactful complement to traditional formats:

- **Polished Introductions:**

AI provides real-time script suggestions and automated editing to ensure professional-quality video resumes.

- **AI-Driven Analytics:**

Recruiters can assess non-verbal cues, such as confidence and communication skills, through AI-powered video analysis.

- ## Advanced Technologies Shaping Resume Building

- **Natural Language Processing (NLP)**

NLP tools summarize long career histories, align job descriptions with skills, and refine language for clarity and impact.

- **Blockchain for Credential Verification**

Blockchain technology enables candidates to securely store and share verified credentials, reducing fraudulent claims and building trust.

- **Voice-Activated Resume Creation**

Future tools will allow job seekers to dictate their resumes, which AI will transcribe and format into professional templates.

- ## Enhanced Personal Branding Through AI

AI tools are assisting candidates in aligning their resumes with their broader personal branding efforts:

- **Consistent Messaging:**

Tools adjust resume tone and style to align with LinkedIn profiles and cover letters.

- **Real-Time Feedback:**

Platforms like Grammarly and Hemingway provide instant suggestions for grammar, style, and tone, ensuring resumes are polished and professional.

• Trends in Recruitment Driven by AI

AI is reshaping how employers evaluate candidates, influencing the way resumes are crafted:

- **Skill Assessments:**

Recruiters increasingly use AI-powered platforms to evaluate skills through simulations and tests. Resumes must align with these assessments by emphasizing relevant abilities.

- **Behavioral Analysis:**

AI tools analyze resumes for tone and personality traits, predicting cultural fit. Candidates should craft resumes that reflect adaptability, leadership, and emotional intelligence.

- **Bias Reduction:**

AI is minimizing unconscious bias by focusing on skills and qualifications instead of demographic details.

• Challenges and Ethical Considerations

While AI offers numerous benefits, challenges remain:

- **Over-Reliance on Automation:**

Generic AI-generated resumes may lack individuality. Job seekers must balance AI assistance with a personal touch.

- **Data Privacy:**

The use of AI and blockchain raises concerns about data security. Candidates must ensure their information is stored securely.

- **Ethical Recruitment Practices:**

Both job seekers and employers should advocate for ethical AI use to prevent algorithmic bias in hiring.

- **Predictions for the Future of Resume Building**

- **Interactive and Visual Storytelling:**
Resumes will evolve into immersive experiences with videos, infographics, and dynamic content.

- **Global Standardization:**

AI-driven templates may lead to a standardized resume format accepted across industries and geographies.

- **Seamless Integration with Recruitment AI:**

Resumes will adapt to complement AI algorithms used by employers, ensuring smooth application processes.

- **Continuous Learning Integration:**

AI tools will sync with platforms like Coursera and Udemy to display completed courses and certifications on resumes.

- **Strategies to Stay Ahead**

- **Leverage AI Tools Effectively:**
Use platforms like Rezi, Jobscan, and Teal for keyword optimization and formatting.

- **Develop Digital Portfolios:**

Integrate resumes with LinkedIn and personal websites for a cohesive professional presence.

- **Focus on Lifelong Learning:**

Regularly upskill and update your resume with new certifications and achievements.

- **Maintain a Balance:**

Combine AI-generated content with a human touch to reflect your unique personality and career trajectory.
By embracing these trends and technologies, job seekers can future-proof their resumes, increase visibility, and enhance their chances of landing their dream roles in an AI-driven job market.

Key Points from Chapter 16: Future Trends in AI and Resume Building

i   AI-Driven Resume Customization:

- Advanced AI tools like Rezi and Jobscan tailor resumes by aligning content with job descriptions, optimizing keyword usage, and generating sections automatically for enhanced ATS compatibility.

ii   Dynamic Portfolios:

- Traditional resumes are being replaced by AI-enabled, real-time updating portfolios that include certifications, projects, and interactive formats such as video introductions and work samples.

iii   Skill Gap Analysis with Predictive Analytics:

- AI platforms like LinkedIn Learning proactively suggest in-demand skills and courses based on industry trends, enabling candidates to remain competitive.

iv   ATS Optimization:

- Tools like Teal and VisualCV refine formatting and keyword usage to ensure resumes effectively pass through ATS filters, a critical step for reaching human recruiters.

v   Visual and Interactive Resumes:

- AI-powered resume builders enhance design with infographics, career timelines, and layout suggestions while maintaining professional readability for various industries.

vi Video Resumes with AI Support:

- AI tools assist in creating polished video resumes by offering real-time script suggestions, automated editing, and non-verbal cue analysis to assess confidence and communication skills.

i Emerging Technologies:

- **NLP**: Summarizes long career histories and aligns job descriptions with skills.
- **Blockchain**: Verifies credentials securely to combat fraudulent claims.
- **Voice-Activated Tools**: Allows dictation of resumes that AI transforms into professional formats.
- **Enhanced Personal Branding**: AI ensures consistent messaging across resumes, LinkedIn profiles, and cover letters, with platforms like Grammarly providing real-time feedback for polished and professional communication.

ii Trends in Recruitment:

- **Skill Assessments**: Recruiters use AI platforms for evaluating specific abilities.
- **Behavioral Analysis**: AI assesses tone and personality traits to predict cultural fit.
- **Bias Reduction**: Focuses on qualifications and skills, reducing unconscious biases in hiring.
- **Ethical and Privacy Challenges**: Over-reliance on AI risks creating generic resumes, while blockchain and other data storage methods highlight the need for stringent data privacy practices and ethical AI use.

iii Future Predictions:

- Interactive resumes will feature videos and dynamic content.
- AI will standardize resume formats globally.

- Seamless integration with recruitment AI will simplify applications.
- Continuous learning platforms will sync directly with resumes to highlight new certifications.

iv Staying Ahead:

- Leverage tools like Rezi and Jobscan for keyword optimization.
- Build dynamic digital portfolios linked to LinkedIn and personal websites.
- Embrace lifelong learning by frequently updating resumes with certifications.
- Balance AI assistance with personal storytelling for a unique, authentic touch.

Module 16 – Quiz

1. **What is a key feature of AI-enabled dynamic portfolios?**
    a. Static formats with fixed data.
    b. Automated updates with new certifications and achievements.
    c. Pre-designed templates without customization options.
    d. Generic formats for all industries.

2. **How does blockchain technology contribute to resume building?**
    a. Helps format resumes for ATS systems.
    b. Verifies credentials to reduce fraud.
    c. Automatically generates personalized resumes.
    d. Replaces traditional job applications.

3. **What is a risk of over-relying on AI for resumes?**
    a. Resumes may appear too creative.
    b. Loss of authenticity and a personal touch.

c. Excessive use of technical jargon.

d. Difficulty passing ATS systems.

4. What AI trend allows candidates to dictate resumes?

a. Predictive analytics.

b. Blockchain integration.

c. Voice-activated resume creation.

d. Natural language processing.

5. Which tool focuses on optimizing resumes for ATS filters?

a. Grammarly.

b. Canva.

c. Jobscan.

d. LinkedIn Learning.

6. What is a common ethical challenge of AI in resume building?

a. AI tools are banned in recruitment processes.

b. Algorithmic bias in hiring decisions.

c. Overcomplicated designs for resumes.

d. Lack of industry-specific features.

Answer Key

1. b. Automated updates with new certifications and achievements.
2. b. Verifies credentials to reduce fraud.
3. b. Loss of authenticity and a personal touch.
4. c. Voice-activated resume creation.
5. c. Jobscan.
6. b. Algorithmic bias in hiring decisions.

in Linkedin
PROFILE OPTAFILE
HEADLINE
EXPERIENCE
SKILLS
HEADLINE
EXPERIENCE
SKILLS
SKILLS
Linkedin
PROFILL

LINKEDIN PROFILE OPTIMIZATION

LinkedIn is the world's largest professional networking platform, essential for career growth and job hunting. With over 900 million users, it serves as a hub for recruiters, professionals, and job seekers. This chapter will guide you through step-by-step optimization of your LinkedIn profile, ensuring it stands out to recruiters and reflects your professional brand effectively.

- **Why LinkedIn is an Essential Tool for Job Seekers**

LinkedIn has transformed professional networking, recruitment, and personal branding. Here's why it's indispensable:

- **Professional Networking**

LinkedIn allows you to connect with industry professionals, thought leaders, and potential mentors globally.

Example: A marketing professional can follow CMOs of leading companies, join marketing groups, and engage with industry-specific content.

- **Job Opportunities**

LinkedIn is a top sourcing tool for recruiters. An optimized profile increases visibility to hiring managers.

Example: A software developer might receive direct outreach from recruiters for new roles.

- **Personal Branding**

Your LinkedIn profile acts as a digital resume and portfolio, showcasing your skills, achievements, and values.

Example: A graphic designer can feature their best work under the "Featured" section for maximum impact.

- **Industry Insights**

Stay updated on trends, news, and advancements by following companies, groups, and thought leaders.

Example: A financial analyst can follow major institutions and read articles to stay informed on market shifts.

- **Skill Development**

LinkedIn Learning offers tailored courses to boost your professional skills.

Example: A project manager can learn Agile methodologies or leadership techniques directly on the platform.

- **Building a Master Resume on LinkedIn**

While job-specific resumes should be tailored, LinkedIn acts as a comprehensive "master resume." Here's how:

- **Work Experience**
- Include all relevant positions with detailed descriptions of responsibilities and achievements.
- Use action verbs and quantify accomplishments for impact.

Example:
Marketing Manager at XYZ Corp (2018-2022)

- Spearheaded digital strategies, increasing organic traffic by 50%.
- Managed a $500K budget, achieving a 20% ROI improvement.
- Led a team of 5 to drive a 150% boost in social media engagement.

- **Education**
- Highlight all degrees, certifications, and notable coursework.
- Include academic honors and leadership roles.

Example:
MBA, Stanford Graduate School of Business (2015-2017)
- Specialization: Digital Marketing
- President, Marketing Club
- Thesis: "The Role of AI in Consumer Behavior."

- **Skills Section**
- Add at least 30 relevant skills for maximum searchability.

Example Skills for Data Scientists: Python, SQL, Data Analysis, Machine Learning, TensorFlow, Tableau.

- **Accomplishments**
- Utilize sections like "Projects," "Publications," and "Certifications."

Example:
Project: Developed a predictive model reducing customer churn by 15%.

- **Optimizing Privacy Settings for Better Visibility**

Privacy settings play a key role in controlling who sees your profile and what they can access. Here's how to optimize them:

- **Enable "Open to Work"**
- Go to your profile and click **Add Profile Section > Intro > Looking for Job Opportunities.**
- Specify roles, locations, and job types.

Pro Tip: Select the option to show this only to recruiters for privacy.

- **Profile Viewing Options**
- Navigate to **Settings > Privacy > Profile Viewing Options.**
- Choose "Public" to maximize recruiter visibility.

- **Manage Connection Visibility**
- Set "Who can see your connections" to "Only Me" to protect your network in competitive industries.

- **Visibility Beyond LinkedIn**
- Turn on "Profile visibility off LinkedIn" to allow search engines to display your profile.

- **Creating an Eye-Catching LinkedIn Banner**

Your banner is prime real estate for personal branding. Here's how to make it impactful:

- **Using Canva to Design a Banner**
- **Visit Canva** and search for "LinkedIn Banner."
- **Choose a Template**: Select one relevant to your profession.

Examples:
- A financial analyst can use charts or graphs.
- A creative professional might opt for vibrant designs.
- **Customize It**: Add your name, title, tagline, and brand colors.
- **Download and Upload**: Save the banner and upload it to LinkedIn.

- **Best Practices for Banners**

- Dimensions: 1584 x 396 pixels.
- Use high-quality, professional visuals.
- Ensure readability on mobile and desktop devices.

- ## Writing an Irresistible Tagline

Your tagline (headline) is critical for visibility and engagement. It appears under your name and influences recruiter search results.

- **Crafting the Best Tagline**
- Highlight your role, expertise, and unique value proposition.

Example:
"Data Scientist | AI Expert | Turning Big Data into Actionable Insights."

- **Dos and Don'ts**

Do:
- Be specific.
- Use industry-relevant keywords.

Don't:
- Use vague terms like "Ninja" or "Guru."
- Overload with punctuation or capitalization.

- **Using AI for Ideas**
- **Prompt**: "Generate 5 taglines for a financial analyst specializing in forecasting and budgeting."

Result:
"Financial Analyst | Strategic Budgeting Expert | Driving Data-Driven Decisions."

- **Selecting the Perfect Profile Picture**

Your profile picture sets the first impression. Here's how to make it professional:

- **Key Guidelines**
- Use high resolution.
- Choose a neutral background.
- Wear professional attire relevant to your industry.

- **Enhancing Photos with Canva**
- Upload your photo to Canva.
- Use the background remover for a clean look.
- Adjust brightness, contrast, and saturation for polish.
- Save and upload to LinkedIn.

- **Crafting a Compelling About Section**

The About section is your professional story. Use this structure:
- **Hook**: Open with a bold statement.

Example: "Award-winning project manager with a passion for delivering transformative results."
- **Middle**: Highlight skills, strengths, and achievements.
- **Conclusion**: End with a call to action.

Pro Tip: Include keywords like "data-driven," "strategic thinker," or "innovator" for SEO.

- **Section-by-Section Profile Optimization**

- **Experience Section**
- Use bullet points to highlight key achievements.

Example:
"Increased sales by 30% through innovative campaigns."

- **Skills Section**
- Add both technical and soft skills.

Example Skills for HR Professionals: Talent Acquisition, Workforce Planning, Conflict Resolution.

- **Certifications**
- Showcase certifications relevant to your industry.

- **Attracting Recruiters to Your Profile**

- **Engage Actively**
- Post content regularly, such as articles, insights, or achievements.

Example: Write about completing a new certification.

- **Join Industry Groups**
- Participate in discussions and share insights in groups like "Project Management Professionals."

- **Leverage LinkedIn Premium**
- Access advanced features like InMail and profile analytics.

- **Final Tips for LinkedIn Success**

- Stay active and consistent to maintain visibility.
- Monitor your profile views and optimize keywords based on analytics.
- Personalize connection requests to build meaningful professional relationships.

By following these steps, your LinkedIn profile will evolve into a dynamic professional tool, making you more discoverable and desirable to recruiters.

Key Points from Chapter 17: LinkedIn Profile Optimization

i Why LinkedIn is Essential for Job Seekers

- **Professional Networking**: Connect globally with industry leaders and peers.
- **Job Opportunities**: Boost visibility to recruiters with an optimized profile.
- **Personal Branding**: Showcase skills and achievements as a digital portfolio.
- **Industry Insights**: Follow companies and thought leaders to stay updated.
- **Skill Development**: Access tailored LinkedIn Learning courses to enhance expertise.

ii Building a Master Resume on LinkedIn

- **Work Experience**: Include detailed roles and quantify achievements (e.g., "Increased traffic by 50%").
- **Education**: Highlight degrees, certifications, and academic accolades.
- **Skills**: Add 30+ relevant skills for searchability (e.g., Python, SQL).
- **Accomplishments**: Showcase projects, publications, and certifications with measurable outcomes.

iii Optimizing Privacy Settings for Visibility

- **Enable "Open to Work"**: Indicate job preferences for recruiters while maintaining privacy.
- **Profile Viewing Options**: Set to "Public" for broader recruiter access.
- **Manage Connection Visibility**: Keep connections private in competitive industries.

- **Visibility Beyond LinkedIn**: Allow search engines to display your profile.

iv Creating an Eye-Catching LinkedIn Banner

- **Designing with Canva**: Create visually appealing banners tailored to your profession.
- Example: Financial analysts can use charts; creative professionals can opt for bold designs.
- **Best Practices**: Use high-quality visuals, professional dimensions (1584 x 396 px), and ensure mobile readability.

v Writing an Irresistible Tagline

- **Crafting Taglines**: Highlight your expertise and unique value proposition (e.g., "Data Scientist | AI Expert | Turning Big Data into Insights").
- **Do's and Don'ts**: Be specific and use keywords, avoiding vague terms or excessive punctuation.
- **AI Assistance**: Use AI prompts to generate engaging taglines.

vi Selecting the Perfect Profile Picture

- **Guidelines**: Use a high-resolution image with a neutral background and professional attire.
- **Enhancing with Canva**: Adjust brightness, contrast, and background for a polished look.

vii Crafting a Compelling About Section

- **Structure**: Hook readers with a bold statement, highlight key achievements, and include a call to action.
- Example: "Award-winning project manager passionate about delivering transformative results."
- **SEO Optimization**: Include industry-relevant keywords (e.g., "strategic thinker").

viii Section-by-Section Profile Optimization

- **Experience**: Use bullet points to focus on measurable outcomes.
- **Skills**: Balance technical and soft skills relevant to your industry.
- **Certifications**: Highlight recent, job-relevant qualifications.

ix Attracting Recruiters to Your Profile

- **Engage Actively**: Post regular updates and achievements.
- **Join Industry Groups**: Participate in discussions to build visibility.
- **Leverage LinkedIn Premium**: Use features like InMail to connect with decision-makers.

x Final Tips for LinkedIn Success

- Stay consistent with activity to maintain visibility.
- Regularly monitor analytics to refine your profile.
- Personalize connection requests to build meaningful relationships.

Module 17 – Quiz

1. **What is the recommended dimension for a LinkedIn banner?**
    a. 1920 x 1080 pixels.
    b. 1584 x 396 pixels.
    c. 1366 x 768 pixels.
    d. 1080 x 1080 pixels.

2. **What section on LinkedIn showcases your achievements visually?**
    a. Education.
    b. Skills.
    c. Featured.
    d. About.

3. **How many skills should you include on your LinkedIn profile?**
    a. 10–15.
    b. At least 30.
    c. 5–10.
    d. Unlimited.

4. **Which of the following is an optimized tagline for LinkedIn?**
    a. Looking for jobs in marketing.
    b. Digital Marketer | SEO Expert | Driving Brand Engagement.
    c. Seeking new opportunities in any field.
    d. Passionate worker open to roles.

5. **What LinkedIn feature should you enable to let recruiters know you're job-seeking?**
   a. Open to Work.
   b. Profile Viewing Options.
   c. Connections Visibility.
   d. Public Activity.

6. **Which tool is recommended for creating a professional LinkedIn banner?**
   a. Grammarly.
   b. Canva.
   c. Jobscan.
   d. HackerRank.

Answer Key

1. b. 1584 x 396 pixels.
2. c. Featured.
3. b. At least 30.
4. b. Digital Marketer | SEO Expert | Driving Brand Engagement.
5. a. Open to Work.
6. b. Canva.

AI
AI-Assisted interview tools
Mock Interview
Mock Interview
AI
Mock Interview
Sessions
Suggested
Answers
Suggested
Answers
Suggest
Result

AI ASSISTED INTERVIEW PREPARATION TOOLS

Objective:

This module equips job seekers with a comprehensive understanding of AI-assisted interviews, provides access to industry-specific tools for mock preparation, and offers actionable strategies to excel in these technologically advanced hiring processes.

Introduction: AI in Interviews

AI-assisted interviews are reshaping the hiring process by enabling employers to evaluate candidates efficiently and objectively. These systems analyze verbal and non-verbal cues, evaluate responses against job-specific requirements, and assess overall candidate suitability. For job seekers, mastering the nuances of these technologies and combining them with traditional preparation techniques is critical for success.

Understanding Country-Specific Interview Patterns

Each country has distinct interview practices shaped by its cultural norms, work ethics, and industry demands. Here's a detailed breakdown of common patterns, specific examples, and preparation strategies:

- **Europe**
- **Interview Pattern:**
- Europe emphasizes scenario-based and behavioral interviews, often requiring structured responses in the STAR format.
- Expect a mix of technical questions, cultural fit assessments, and competency-based queries.
- Example: "Describe a time when you handled a project delay" (answered using STAR).

- **How to Prepare:**
- Analyze the job description (JD) and highlight the key competencies required.
- Prepare 5–7 case studies or scenarios showcasing your experience using STAR:
  - **Situation:** The context.
  - **Task:** Your responsibility.
  - **Action:** Steps you took.
  - **Result:** The outcome.

- **Recommended Tools:**
- **Interview Query** for tailored role-based scenarios.
- **Big Interview** to refine responses for cultural fit and stakeholder engagement.

- **India**
- **Interview Pattern:**
- Indian interviews typically involve a combination of technical, HR, and managerial rounds.
- Expect aptitude tests, domain-specific questions, and situational problem-solving.
- Example: "How would you resolve a conflict between team members?"

- **How to Prepare:**
- Focus on domain knowledge, as technical expertise is often a priority.
- Review your JD and CV to align examples with the role's key requirements.
- Use practice tools to prepare for numerical and logical reasoning tests.

- **Recommended Tools:**
- **HackerRank** for coding and technical skills.
- **PrepInsta** for aptitude test preparation.

- **United States**
- **Interview Pattern:**
- U.S. interviews emphasize storytelling, leadership qualities, and alignment with company culture.
- Behavioral and competency-based questions are common, alongside assessments of innovation and problem-solving.
- Example: "Tell me about a time you demonstrated leadership in a challenging situation."

- **How to Prepare:**
- Research the company's mission, values, and culture using Glassdoor or LinkedIn.
- Practice storytelling techniques that highlight accomplishments and leadership.
- Prepare quantifiable examples that show measurable results.

- **Recommended Tools:**
- **Big Interview** for practicing situational responses.
- **Yoodli** to improve communication and presentation skills.

- **Australia**
- **Interview Pattern:**
- Australian interviews value straightforward communication and adaptability.
- Expect scenario-based questions that assess decision-making and collaboration.
- Example: "Describe how you handled a project that required working across multiple teams."
- **How to Prepare:**
- Highlight your adaptability and teamwork skills.
- Use the JD to identify key attributes and prepare examples showcasing resourcefulness.

- **Recommended Tools:**
- **Interview360** for role-specific scenarios and feedback.
- **PracticeMock** for behavioral questions.

- **Germany**
- **Interview Pattern:**
- German interviews are highly structured and technical, often involving panel interviews and problem-solving exercises.
- Cultural fit and precision are key, with questions designed to assess technical expertise and logical thinking.
- Example: "How would you optimize this process to reduce inefficiencies?"

- **How to Prepare:**
- Focus on precision and technical accuracy in your responses.
- Be prepared for industry-specific technical tests or case studies.
- Research the company's processes and tailor your examples accordingly.

- **Recommended Tools:**
- **CodeSignal** for technical assessments.
- **Interviewing.io** for mock technical interviews with industry professionals.

Steps for Maximizing Preparation

Regardless of location, successful interview preparation requires a structured approach:
- **Analyze the Job Description (JD):**
- Extract important keywords and skills.
- Identify themes such as technical expertise, leadership, or communication.

- **Craft Tailored Case Studies:**
- For each keyword, prepare STAR-based examples that showcase relevant experience.
- Link your examples to your CV and ensure alignment with the JD.

- **Leverage Multiple Tools:**
- Use general AI platforms (e.g., ChatGPT) for broad insights.
- Transition to role-specific tools (e.g., CodeSignal for coding or Yoodli for communication).

- **Practice Behavioral and Situational Responses:**
- Record your answers to evaluate tone, clarity, and body language.
- Focus on delivering concise, structured, and impactful responses.

- **Focus on Non-Verbal Communication:**
- Practice maintaining eye contact, using appropriate gestures, and modulating tone.

- **Prepare Your Environment:**
- Ensure a distraction-free setup with a professional background.

How AI Helps in Interview Preparation

AI has revolutionized the way candidates prepare for interviews by providing personalized insights, replicating real-world scenarios, and enhancing overall readiness. Here's how AI tools contribute:

- **Tailored Feedback:**

AI tools analyze speech, tone, body language, and content delivery to provide actionable feedback.
Example: Tools like HireVue or Yoodli help candidates refine clarity, confidence, and conciseness.

- **Scenario Simulations:**

Platforms simulate realistic interview scenarios, from technical tests to behavioral assessments.
Example: PracticeMock offers specialty-focused simulations for medical professionals, while LeetCode Wizard targets software development.

- **Keyword Optimization:**

AI highlights important keywords from job descriptions, ensuring alignment in resumes and interview responses.
Example: AIApply generates interview questions based on job descriptions.

- **Behavioral Insights:**

AI tools assess non-verbal cues like posture, eye contact, and expressions to provide behavioral feedback.

Example: Interview360 evaluates emotional intelligence and engagement.

The Risks of Over-Dependence on AI

While AI offers immense benefits, relying on it excessively can have drawbacks:

- Loss of Authenticity:
  Over-preparation may lead to rehearsed, robotic answers, which can diminish genuine engagement during live interviews.
- Limited Adaptability:
  AI tools cannot replicate human intuition or cultural understanding, which are critical in real-time interactions.
- Generalized Feedback:
  AI often provides standard suggestions, which may not address niche requirements of specific roles.
- Reduced Critical Thinking:
  Depending on AI-generated responses can hinder a candidate's ability to think spontaneously and adapt to unexpected questions.

Why Specific Tools Are Better Than ChatGPT and Perplexity

General AI tools like ChatGPT and Perplexity provide broad insights, but role-specific tools deliver precise, actionable preparation:

- **Role-Specific Scenarios:**

Tools like Interview Query for data scientists or Big Interview for L&D professionals tailor their content to industry needs.

- **Real-Time Feedback:**

Platforms such as Yoodli analyze delivery style, tone, and clarity, offering more targeted feedback than general AI tools.

- **Hands-On Practice:**

Platforms like CodeSignal or HackerRank simulate coding challenges, which ChatGPT cannot replicate interactively.

- **Blended AI-Human Feedback:**

Tools like Interviewing.io combine AI insights with professional guidance, ensuring comprehensive preparation.

Glassdoor: A Treasure Trove for Interview Preparation

Glassdoor is a valuable resource for understanding company-specific interview processes, commonly asked questions, and employer expectations. Here's how to use it effectively:

Steps to Use Glassdoor:

- **Search for the Company:**

Enter the company name and access the "Interviews" section. *Example:* Searching "Amazon Data Scientist" provides insights into interview formats.

- **Filter by Job Title:**

Use filters to refine results based on specific roles, such as "Software Engineer" or "Business Analyst."

- **Explore Interview Questions:**

Identify recurring themes in candidate-reported questions. *Example:* Behavioral questions like "Describe a time you resolved a conflict" can be prepared using the STAR format.

- **Review Candidate Experiences:**

Study feedback on interview stages, difficulty levels, and assessment tools used.
Example: If candidates mention coding challenges via HackerRank, include that in your preparation.

- **Understand Employer Expectations:**

Learn what qualities the company prioritizes and tailor your answers accordingly.
Example: If problem-solving is emphasized, prepare examples that highlight analytical skills.

Can You Prepare for the Same Interview on Multiple Platforms?

Yes, using multiple platforms enhances preparation but requires a strategic approach:

- **Start Broad:**

Use general AI platforms like ChatGPT to gather insights on common questions and company profiles.

- **Go Deep:**

Transition to role-specific tools for detailed practice. For example:
- Yoodli for communication skills.
- CodeSignal for technical challenges.
- Big Interview for situational responses.

- **Consolidate Feedback:**

Practice the same questions across different tools to gain varied perspectives, but synthesize learnings to avoid redundancy.

- **Focus on Quality Over Quantity:**

Prioritize mastering a few tools rather than spreading efforts too thin.

AI Mock Interview Tools by Profession

Here's a detailed breakdown of AI tools tailored to specific roles, including descriptions, ease of use, pricing, unique selling points (USPs), and drawbacks.

- **Learning and Development (L&D) Professionals**

Tool: Interview360 by The Access Group
- Description: A comprehensive AI-powered platform offering tailored scenarios and feedback for L&D professionals. Designed to help candidates refine communication and training design strategies.
- Ease of Use: Intuitive interface; users can upload resumes and receive personalized interview simulations.
- Pricing: Custom pricing for organizations; individuals need organizational access.
- USP: Personalized scenarios aligned with corporate L&D roles and real-time body language analysis.
- Drawback: Limited accessibility for individuals without organizational subscriptions.

Tool: HireVue
- Description: One of the most widely used platforms for AI-powered video interviews, focusing on tone analysis, facial expressions, and real-time feedback.
- Ease of Use: Very user-friendly, but candidates must follow structured guidelines during recordings.
- Pricing: Organization-licensed, typically not available for personal use.
- USP: Realistic simulations aligned with actual corporate hiring practices.

- Drawback: Misinterpretation of accents or cultural differences may impact feedback accuracy.

Tool: Big Interview

- Description: A platform offering mock interviews specifically for soft skills, situational responses, and behavioral questions in L&D roles.
- Ease of Use: Straightforward; includes tutorials and guided exercises.
- Pricing: $79/year for individual users.
- USP: Comprehensive training for role-specific scenarios with a focus on stakeholder engagement.
- Drawback: Requires significant time investment to fully utilize its features.

- **Data Science Professionals**

Tool: Pramp

- Description: A peer-to-peer platform where candidates can practice technical and coding challenges with real-time problem-solving.
- Ease of Use: Simple to navigate; users are matched with peers for live practice sessions.
- Pricing: Free.
- USP: Offers a collaborative approach to technical interviews, enabling candidates to learn from peers.
- Drawback: Feedback quality depends on the peer's expertise and skill level.

Tool: CodeSignal

- Description: An AI-driven assessment tool with coding challenges for data science roles, including Python, R, and SQL tests.
- Ease of Use: User-friendly with a clean, interactive coding environment.
- Pricing: Starts at $20/month.

- USP: Mimics real-world scenarios, making it highly relevant for data-centric roles.
- Drawback: Focuses primarily on technical skills, with little emphasis on soft skills or behavioral responses.

Tool: Interview Query

- Description: A tool specifically designed for data scientists, offering industry-specific mock interview questions and instant feedback.
- Ease of Use: Requires some familiarity with technical terminology; guided tutorials are available.
- Pricing: $49/month.
- USP: Tailored questions for machine learning, data analysis, and statistical modeling.
- Drawback: Limited non-technical preparation, such as communication or behavioral skill enhancement.

- **Software Developers**

Tool: LeetCode Wizard

- Description: A widely used platform for practicing coding algorithms and technical challenges, catering to software engineers.
- Ease of Use: Easy to navigate with detailed explanations for each problem.
- Pricing: Free basic version; premium plans start at $35/month.
- USP: Robust library of algorithm-based problems with multi-language support.
- Drawback: Focuses solely on coding challenges, leaving out soft skills and communication training.

Tool: HackerRank

- Description: A platform that offers coding libraries and interactive challenges tailored to technical interviews.
- Ease of Use: Intuitive and beginner-friendly, with tutorials for complex problems.

- Pricing: Free for individuals; premium starts at $25/month.
- USP: Extensive coding practice with real-time feedback and scoring.
- Drawback: Minimal focus on behavioral and situational questions.

Tool: Interviewing.io

- Description: Allows candidates to conduct mock interviews with experienced engineers from top tech companies.
- Ease of Use: Simple to book sessions; integrates feedback seamlessly into user dashboards.
- Pricing: Free for initial sessions; premium options vary.
- USP: Provides insights and advice directly from industry professionals.
- Drawback: Limited availability due to high demand, making it harder to schedule sessions.

- **Business Analysts**

Tool: Yoodli

- Description: AI-driven platform focusing on communication and presentation skills, helping BAs articulate complex concepts effectively.
- Ease of Use: Highly user-friendly, with instant feedback on speech clarity and delivery.
- Pricing: Free basic version; premium plans available.
- USP: Enhances articulation and builds confidence for presenting data-driven insights.
- Drawback: Limited technical or case-based scenario training.

Tool: Jobma

- Description: A video interview tool designed for analytical and problem-solving scenarios in business roles.
- Ease of Use: Easy setup with guided interview simulations.
- Pricing: Starts at $30/month.

- USP: Simulated business-specific questions and communication analysis.
- Drawback: Generic feedback that may not fully capture the nuances of BA roles.

Tool: PrepInsta

- Description: Offers mock interviews and aptitude tests for decision-making and analytical roles.
- Ease of Use: Beginner-friendly with simple navigation and mock test access.
- Pricing: $15/month.
- USP: Focuses on real-world decision-making scenarios and business acumen tests.
- Drawback: Limited depth for highly advanced or niche BA interviews.

- **Chartered Accountants**

Tool: VMock

- Description: An AI-powered tool providing detailed feedback on resumes and interview performance, tailored for finance professionals.
- Ease of Use: Straightforward, with automated feedback within minutes.
- Pricing: $29/month.
- USP: Highlights critical areas for improvement in finance-specific interviews.
- Drawback: Generic advice for specialized accounting topics.

Tool: AIApply

- Description: A customizable interview preparation tool that generates questions based on job descriptions.
- Ease of Use: Simple and quick setup with job description upload functionality.
- Pricing: Free basic version; premium plans not specified.

- USP: Personalized question generation and adaptability to diverse accounting scenarios.
- Drawback: Limited depth in niche accounting fields like international taxation.

Tool: Zeteo

- Description: Focuses on case-study-based interview scenarios for accounting professionals.
- Ease of Use: Interactive and easy to navigate.
- Pricing: Free trial; premium starts at $50/month.
- USP: Real-world case studies relevant to accounting roles.
- Drawback: May not cover global financial frameworks comprehensively.

- **Doctors (Any Specialty)**

Tool: PracticeMock

- Description: Offers interactive mock interviews tailored for various medical specialties.
- Ease of Use: Simple to set up; users can select specialty-specific scenarios.
- Pricing: $15/month.
- USP: Adapts scenarios based on specialty, providing targeted preparation.
- Drawback: Limited coverage for global or highly niche medical practices.

Tool: Bemo Academic Consulting

- Description: Designed for high-stakes medical interviews, with a focus on ethical dilemmas and situational judgment.
- Ease of Use: Requires moderate familiarity with medical interview formats.
- Pricing: $297/session.
- USP: Comprehensive and tailored for high-pressure scenarios like residency interviews.
- Drawback: Expensive, making it less accessible for all candidates.

Tool: iPrepDental

- Description: Specially designed for dental professionals, focusing on practical and ethical scenarios.
- Ease of Use: User-friendly, with guided practice sessions.
- Pricing: $25/session.
- USP: Dentistry-specific questions with interactive mock interview functionality.
- Drawback: Narrow focus, applicable only to dental roles.

Strategies Beyond AI Tools

Preparation for AI-assisted interviews must balance technology with traditional techniques:

- **Understand the Job Description (JD):**

Identify key skills and prepare examples using the STAR (Situation, Task, Action, Result) method.

- **Research the Company:**

Dive deep into the company's mission, values, and recent projects. Use Glassdoor and LinkedIn for additional insights.

- **Refine Your LinkedIn Profile:**

Align your profile with the job description by emphasizing relevant skills and accomplishments.

- **Practice Non-Verbal Communication:**

Record responses to evaluate body language, tone, and eye contact.

- **Prepare Your Environment:**

Set up a distraction-free space with a professional background and test your internet connection.

- **Post-Interview Follow-Up:**

Send a thank-you email that reiterates your interest and reflects on specific points discussed during the interview.

Conclusion

AI-assisted interviews demand a balanced approach, combining technological preparation with traditional strategies. By leveraging specialized tools, using resources like Glassdoor, and maintaining authenticity, candidates can confidently navigate the evolving landscape of hiring processes.

Key Points from Chapter 18: AI-Assisted Interview Preparation Tools

i The Role of AI in Interviews

- AI analyzes verbal and non-verbal cues for efficient evaluation.
- Aligns responses with job-specific requirements to assess suitability.
- Enhances preparation and readiness through advanced tools.

ii How AI Tools Assist in Interview Preparation

- **Tailored Feedback**: Tools like HireVue and Yoodli refine speech, tone, and body language.
- **Scenario Simulations**: Platforms such as PracticeMock replicate real-world interview formats.
- **Keyword Optimization**: AIApply generates questions aligned with job descriptions.
- **Behavioral Insights**: Interview360 evaluates emotional intelligence and engagement.

iii Risks of Over-Reliance on AI

- **Loss of Authenticity**: Robotic responses can diminish genuine engagement.
- **Limited Adaptability**: AI lacks human intuition for real-time interactions.
- **Generic Feedback**: Standardized insights may not suit niche roles.
- **Reduced Spontaneity**: Overuse of AI can hinder on-the-spot thinking.

iv **Advantages of Role-Specific Tools Over General AI Platforms**

- **Targeted Scenarios**: Tools like Interview Query and Big Interview cater to industry needs.
- **Real-Time Feedback**: Yoodli enhances delivery style and tone.
- **Hands-On Practice**: CodeSignal provides interactive coding simulations.
- **Blended Feedback**: Interviewing.io combines AI analysis with expert guidance.

v **Using Glassdoor for Interview Preparation**

- **Search and Filter**: Access company-specific insights and role-related questions.
- **Identify Patterns**: Recognize recurring questions and focus areas.
- **Understand Expectations**: Tailor responses to employer priorities.
- **Leverage Peer Experiences**: Study feedback on interview formats and difficulty.

vi **Maximizing Multiple Preparation Platforms**

- **Start Broad**: Use general tools like ChatGPT for foundational insights.
- **Transition to Specialized Tools**: Focus on role-specific preparation with targeted platforms.
- **Consolidate Feedback**: Synthesize inputs from multiple tools for clarity.
- **Focus on High-Impact Tools**: Prioritize mastering a few over spreading efforts thin.

vii Top AI Mock Interview Tools by Profession

- **Learning and Development Professionals**: Interview360, HireVue, Big Interview.
- **Data Science Professionals**: Pramp, CodeSignal, Interview Query.
- **Software Developers**: LeetCode Wizard, HackerRank, Interviewing.io.
- **Business Analysts**: Yoodli, Jobma, PrepInsta.
- **Chartered Accountants**: VMock, AIApply, Zeteo.
- **Doctors**: PracticeMock, Bemo Academic Consulting, iPrepDental.

viii Strategies Beyond AI Tools

- **Understand the Job Description**: Use the STAR method for examples.
- **Research the Company**: Dive into mission, values, and recent projects.
- **Refine Non-Verbal Skills**: Practice tone, posture, and eye contact.
- **Prepare the Environment**: Ensure a distraction-free, professional setup.
- **Follow Up**: Send a thank-you email reinforcing key points discussed.

Module 18 – Quiz

1. **What does the STAR method stand for?**
    a. Situation, Task, Action, Result.
    b. Solution, Task, Activity, Result.
    c. Strategy, Target, Action, Review.
    d. Situation, Time, Achievement, Response.

2. **Which tool offers real-time feedback on tone and delivery during interviews?**
    a. Glassdoor.
    b. Yoodli.
    c. Grammarly.
    d. Canva.

3. **What is the main advantage of using Glassdoor for interview preparation?**
    a. Helps with resume formatting.
    b. Provides company-specific insights and commonly asked questions.
    c. Automates the application process.
    d. Evaluates non-verbal communication skills.

4. **Which platform combines AI insights with expert feedback for mock interviews?**
    a. Big Interview.
    b. Interviewing.io.
    c. PrepInsta.
    d. HireVue.

5. **Which AI tool is most suited for technical interviews for software developers?**
   a. HackerRank.
   b. Canva.
   c. Jobscan.
   d. Glassdoor.

6. **What is a potential risk of over-reliance on AI during interview preparation?**
   a. Increased confidence during interviews.
   b. Reduced adaptability and spontaneity.
   c. Stronger alignment with job requirements.
   d. Improved communication skills.

Answer Key

1. a. Situation, Task, Action, Result.
2. b. Yoodli.
3. b. Provides company-specific insights and commonly asked questions.
4. b. Interviewing.io.
5. a. HackerRank.
6. b. Reduced adaptability and spontaneity.

CONCLUSION: EMPOWERING YOUR CAREER WITH AI AND HUMAN INGENUITY

As you turn the final page of this book, you stand equipped with the tools, insights, and strategies to craft a resume that doesn't just pass an ATS but captivates human recruiters. The journey from confusion and rejection to clarity and confidence is not without effort, but every step forward is a testament to your growth and determination.

Through these 18 chapters, we've explored the transformative potential of AI in resume building, blending it seamlessly with the irreplaceable human touch. From understanding ATS strategies and mastering personal summaries to harnessing AI tools for cover letters and interview preparation, this guide has been designed to empower you every step of the way.

Failures and challenges will inevitably arise, but let them serve as opportunities for learning and improvement. The dynamic world of job searching demands adaptability, and you now hold the knowledge to navigate it with confidence.

This book is more than just a resource—it's a call to action. Apply what you've learned, embrace innovation, and never lose sight of your unique value. Whether you are crafting your next resume, acing an interview, or envisioning the career of your dreams, know that your effort and perseverance will pave the way to success.

Thank you for allowing me to be a part of your journey. Now, it's your turn to take charge and create the future you deserve.

THANK YOU TO ALL MY READERS

To all my readers, thank you for allowing this book to be a part of your journey. Your time and trust in these pages mean the world to me. My hope is that the strategies, tools, and insights shared here will guide you toward achieving your career aspirations.
Remember, every challenge you face is a step forward, and your growth lies in the perseverance to overcome it. Wishing you success, fulfilment, and the confidence to build the future you deserve.

With gratitude,
Aparajita Sudarshan

DISCLAIMER

This book is intended as a guide to help readers navigate the complexities of resume building and job searching by utilizing AI tools and strategies. While I have provided AI prompts, techniques, and content to the best of my ability, I do not guarantee job placements, interviews, or specific outcomes. The effectiveness of the tools and strategies discussed will depend on individual circumstances and efforts.
The mention of websites, platforms, and AI tools throughout this book is for informational purposes only. These references are based on publicly available information, and I am not affiliated with or endorsing any specific platform or service.
My sole objective is to bring forward the potential of AI tools and provide readers with practical insights to improve their job search strategies.
Readers are encouraged to use their judgment and adapt the techniques shared here to their unique needs. The information provided is meant to empower, not replace, personal effort, creativity, and critical thinking in crafting resumes and navigating the job market.

SOURCES

The content and insights presented in this book are based on a combination of my knowledge, experience, and extensive research. Various tools and platforms were explored to provide accurate and actionable information, including **ChatGPT**, **Perplexity**, **Claude**, **Google**, and publicly available data from job boards and websites.

While these sources were instrumental in shaping the prompts, strategies, and examples shared, the content has been carefully tailored and uniquely written to ensure originality and relevance. This book is not affiliated with or endorsed by any of the mentioned platforms. My goal is to guide readers toward making the most of AI tools and resources available in the public domain for their professional growth.

By synthesizing information from these platforms and combining it with personal insights, this book aims to offer a practical, ethical, and actionable framework for leveraging AI in resume building and job searches.